HOLD ON TO HOPE

SUGGESTIONS FOR LDS CODEPENDENTS

Hold On To Hope

Suggestions for LDS Codependents

Compiled by Hidden Treasures

Copyright © 1993 by Hidden Treasures

ALL RIGHTS RESERVED.

No part of this book may be reproduced in any form whatsoever, whether by graphic, visual, electronic, filming, microfilming, tape recording, or any other means, without the prior written permission of the author, except in the case of brief passages embodied in critical reviews and articles.

This book is not an official publication of The Church of Jesus Christ of Latter-day Saints. All material herein is the responsibility of the author and not of the publisher or of The Church of Jesus Christ of Latter-day Saints.

This book is not intended to replace the advice of a mental health professional. Readers who are currently involved with counceling should consider the text as a supplemental resource only. Individuals ought not to make major changes in their lives without first consulting their therapist or physician.

ISBN: 1-55517-119-2
Library of Congress Catalog Card Number: 93-72498

Published and distributed by:

CFI
Cedar Fort, Incorporated
925 North Main, Springville, UT 84663   801-489-4084

Cover Design by Lyle Mortimer
Typeset by Brian Carter
Lithographed in the United States of America

TABLE OF CONTENTS

Introduction vii

1. The Addiction Cycle 1
    First Stage 3
    Second Stage 7
    Third Stage 12
    Recovery Stage 16

2. Hi! I'm Tony and I'm an Alcoholic
    (A Personal Story of Addiction) 19

3. The LDS Family Adjusting to Addiction 27
    Rescuing Behaviors 29
    Persecuting Behaviors 32
    Suffering Behaviors 34
    Adjusting to Addiction Chart 38

4. Without Love (A Personal Story of an Alcoholic Parent)
    By Vaughn J. Featherstone 39

5. In the Name of Love
    (A Personal Story of Codependence) 45

6. Self-Love 53
    The Love Formula 55
    A Model of Self-Love 57
    Self-Love Meter 59
    Emotional and Spiritual Self-Reliance 61
    How Does One Develop Self-Love? 64

7. Unconditional Love 73
    The Good Samaritan 73

　　　　Personalities Before Principles.. 74
　　　　How Does One Develop Unconditional Love? 78
　　　　Hold On with an Open Hand.. 85

8. Tough Love.. 89
　　　　The Prodigal Son 90
　　　　The Refiner's Fire... 92
　　　　How Does One Develop Tough Love?............................... 96
　　　　What Tough Love is Not... 100
　　　　Recovering from Codependence Chart 104

9. Bringing It Together 105
　　　　Strategies 105
　　　　How Does One Develop Strategies?................................... 108
　　　　God's Kind of Love-Chart 112
　　　　Hints for Effective Strategies.. 115
　　　　The Sunbeam Check 119

10. Suggestions and Afterthoughts
　　　By Vaughn J. Featherstone... 123

Appendix A
　　　Resources.. 131

Index 135

INTRODUCTION

HOLD ON TO HOPE: Suggestions for LDS Codependents was compiled by Hidden Treasures. This book brings together the material of four authors and addresses those families who have a problem with addiction. Its purpose is twofold: first, to offer individuals suggestions on how to care for themselves and, second, to provide them with ideas of how to effectively intervene in the life of an addict.

The first author, Dr. Rick H., is a successful lecturer and psychologist. He contributes the bulk of material that makes up this book. A specialist in the field of addiction for more than fifteen years, he now shares his lecture notes. In Chapter One Dr. Rick begins by explaining the addiction process and assists families in understanding the disease concept and the loss of free agency that occurs with substance misuse. Chapter Three discusses in detail the various codependent behaviors that are embraced by surrounding loved ones in an effort to deal with the substance abuser. True stories are interwoven with the lecture material to illustrate the various concepts. Readers will gain maximum benefit as they read the educational material and the subsequent chapters which provide personal experiences.

Chapter Two, *Hi! I'm Tony and I'm an Alcoholic*, tells the story of a Mormon alcoholic and Chapter Five, *In the Name of Love*, is the personal story of Tony's wife. Names have been changed or not used to secure anonymity.

Vaughn J. Featherstone contributes Chapters Four and Ten. Readers will recognize the rare opportunity to learn from this beloved General Authority's personal story. In *Without Love*, Elder Featherstone offers the reader hope by recalling his experience growing up in an alcoholic home. And in *Suggestions and Afterthoughts*, he provides suggestions for those who deal with addicts.

The word "addict" is used throughout the book in reference to those individuals who have progressed so far in the use of a substance that they have lost control. This loss of control is often referred to as "addiction" or "a disease." There are many substances to which people become "addicted." Common addictions include alcohol, drugs, and food, but other things can also lead to addiction-entertaining lustful thoughts and spending money for example. The word "codependent" is used to identify those individuals who develop selected behaviors as they adjust to another individual becoming an addict.

There is a misconception that you can do nothing with addicts until they ask for help and "hit bottom." Waiting for addicts to gain spontaneous insight into their addictions is evidence of a gross misunderstanding about the nature of addiction. The belief of doing nothing until the addict hits bottom is dangerous. Help for the addict almost always comes from someone besides the addict. Simply said, those who are the victims of addiction are incapable of recognizing the severity of their symptoms. Denial is part of the disease. The use of strategies and interventions should be the norm rather than the exception. *HOLD ON TO HOPE* offers suggestions on how to intervene. The book uses a unique approach as it introduces gospel principles to the intervention process.

CHAPTER ONE

THE ADDICTION CYCLE

I once heard a speaker say, "Blessed is he that believes, but more blessed is he that knows why he believes." The purpose of this discussion is to help the reader understand *why* it is important to obey the Word of Wisdom and the Law of Chastity. A surprising number of LDS Church members believe the major reason to abstain from drugs, alcohol, and immoral sexual behavior is because of the negative physical, legal, and emotional consequences. Typically, members discuss negative consequences such as poor health, jail time, suicide, birth defects, sexually transmitted diseases, and the like. However, the Lord clearly reminds us that all laws and commandments are spiritual in nature.

> Wherefore, verily I say unto you that all things unto me are spiritual, and not at any time have I given unto you a law which was temporal; neither any man, nor the children of men, neither Adam, your father, whom I created. Behold, I gave unto him that he should be an agent unto himself; and I gave unto him commandment, but no temporal commandment gave I unto him, for my commandments are spiritual; they are not natural nor temporal, neither carnal nor sensual. (D&C 29:34-35)

Elder Stephen L. Richards further illustrates the spiritual nature of commandments in this discussion about the Word of Wisdom.

> Every commandment of God is spiritual in nature.... The Word of Wisdom is spiritual. It is true that it enjoins the use of deleterious substances and makes provision for the health of the body. But the largest measure of good derived from its observance is in increased faith and the development of more spiritual power and wisdom. Likewise, the most regrettable and damaging effects of its infractions are spiritual, also. Injury to the body may be comparatively trivial to the damage to the soul in the destruction of faith and the retardation of spiritual growth. So I say, every commandment involves a spiritual growth. (Stephen L.

Richards, in Conference Report, Apr. 1949, p. 141. © Copyright by The Church of Jesus Christ of Latter-day Saints. Used by permission.)

A quote from President Benson also teaches this concept.

> I have always felt...that the greater blessing of obedience to the Word of Wisdom and all other commandments is spiritual....My young brothers and sisters, in all love, we give you warning that Satan and his emissaries will strive to entice you to use harmful substances, because they well know if you partake, your spiritual powers will be inhibited and you will be in their evil power. (President Ezra Taft Benson April 3, 1983, *Ensign* © Copyright by The Church of Jesus Christ of Latter-day Saints. Used by permission.)

First use of alcohol and drugs or involvement with immoral behavior rarely brings physical tragedy. Typically the individual doing the behavior does not get arrested, does not go to jail, does not go to the hospital, does not get any disease, and does not lose his mind or die. Often, the first misuse of substances is not even detected by parents or even a spouse. With drugs, for example, a headache or a side ache might be the ultimate displeasure. At times, a beginning marijuana user experiences no effects or perhaps simply falls asleep. It is interesting to note that in over 15 years of drug counseling, the side ache is one of the most common complaints for the initial marijuana user. When asked about side aches users often reply: "I laughed so hard while high that my ribs hurt!" This is not to say that adverse consequences never occur after only one use or one immoral act. A single use of a drug like PCP can be disastrous, and the addiction potential for a person smoking Crack is tremendous. Certainly, one can be exposed to AIDS during a first sexual encounter. In summary, most first-time users do *not* experience physical *pain*. Rather, an individual involved in addictive behavior will feel a form of *pleasure*. Let's look carefully at an LDS model of addiction.

FIRST STAGE OF ADDICTION

Much research has been done and numerous theories are available which explain various addiction cycles. Perhaps the easiest to understand is the cycle once used by the LDS Church Welfare Department in training missionaries assigned to areas of the world with a high rate of alcoholism. The addiction cycle is discussed in three stages, the first stage of alcohol or drug use being one of joy or pleasure, as depicted in the figure below.

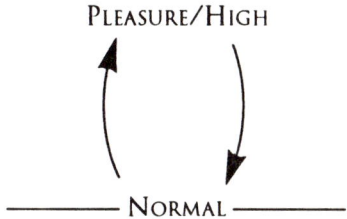

The user discovers a form of joy (pleasure or "a high") associated with substance use. These substances may be alcohol, drugs, or even pornography. An important thing to remember is that these substances are effective and dependable. Their use by almost anyone will typically influence the way that person feels, usually in a pleasurable fashion. In 3 Nephi 27:11 Jesus says that whether we build our lives "...*upon the works of men, or upon the works of the devil...[we shall] have joy in [our] works for a season...*" It would appear obvious that alcohol and drug abuse arise from "...*evils and designs which do and will exist in the hearts of conspiring men in the last days...*" (D&C 89:4). These scriptures suggest that those who abuse substances are building their lives upon the "works of men or upon the works of the devil."

Therefore, we can logically assume, according to Book of Mormon scripture, that beginning substance users *will have joy*-or a form thereof-during their first stage of use.

As mentioned, a person's first experience with a substance is usually pleasant and gives him or her a feeling of wellbeing and peace. As the effects of the substance wear off, the user returns to normal, with no evidence of harm. Because of the pleasure experienced, substance users begin to doubt the warnings they have heard from parents and Church leaders. Imagine what might be said among a group of teens about using alcohol or drugs, or viewing pornography. The conversation would likely contain comments such as "Wow!" "Let's go get high." "That'll be fun." "Where's the party?" "Will Betty be there?" These teens would not likely say of such activities: "That sounds boring." "Someone will get arrested." "Someone could get killed."

Historically, risk factors such as low self-esteem, broken families and physical abuse have been listed as problems that predispose a person to misuse substances. In addition to traditional risk factors, a recent trend in predicting substance misuse, at least for teenagers, includes peer pressure and curiosity. These risk factors are experienced by most and surely place LDS persons equally at risk for misuse of substances.

Substance misuse, in the first stage of addiction could be considered a sin. This is true because most of us have the ability to stop at this stage. The pleasure one derives "for a season" is a sign of this first stage of addiction and is a common element of all addictions.

SPIRITUAL RUIN

One might ask, "What's the big deal about drinking just a small amount of beer? or smoking a little pot? or making out with someone you really care for?" The answers are found in the scriptures and quotes discussed above, which suggest that one's spirituality is threatened even with first use. That is, the beginning of *spiritual ruin* is the greatest danger in the first stage of addiction, *not* physical destruction.

A similar concept exists for other types of addiction. The gambler rarely loses his life's fortune on the first bet. He usually begins with small wagers and experiences the "pleasure" associated with occasional winning. For the sex addict, the first stage of addiction may involve "soft pornography" viewed privately without any obvious negative consequences. Negative temporal consequences rarely occur during the first stage of most addictions. A small twinge of guilt for having been disobedient to a spiritual commandment may be the only price paid by the naive user during the first stage of addiction. This twinge of guilt can be likened to planting a seed.

The commandments governing our code of conduct are usually well taught in the early years of Church attendance and are reinforced by individuals periodically committing themselves to comply. Elder G. Smith discusses the Word of Wisdom in the following quote:

> And all saints who remember to keep and do these saying walking in obedience to the commandments.... (D&C 89:18) This means all the commandments, including tithes and offerings, Sabbath day, sacrament meetings, etc. Then he adds the promise of the blessings of health. Then adds this promise: And shall find wisdom and great treasures of knowledge, even hidden treasures. (D&C 89:19)
>
> What is a more hidden treasure than a testimony of the divinity of the gospel of Jesus Christ? This comes as a result of obedience to the laws of God, not just because we have good health. I have heard many converts tell how they learned to live the Word of Wisdom to join the Church. Good health is not a requirement to join the Church. Obedience is. Each one has said if that's what the Lord wanted, he would do it. (Conference Report, Oct. 1970, p. 16; or Improvement Era, Dec. 1970, p. 42. © Copyright by The Church of Jesus Christ of Latter-day Saints. Used by permission.)

As the LDS substance user begins alcohol and drug use or immoral behavior disobedience always occurs because of promises made at baptism and the probable years of Church instruction in such places as Sunday School, home, and seminary. Spiritual decline begins through disobedience to a fundamental teaching. King Benjamin explains what happens when a member of the Church disobeys a commandment like the Word of Wisdom or the Law of Chastity.

> And now, I say unto you, my brethren, that after ye have known and have been taught all these things, if ye should transgress and go contrary to that which has been spoken, that ye do withdraw yourselves from the Spirit of the Lord that it may have no place in you to guide you in wisdom's paths that ye may be blessed, prospered, and preserved- I say unto you, that the man that doeth this, the same cometh out in open rebellion against God; therefore he listeth to obey the evil spirit, and becometh an enemy to all righteousness; therefore, the Lord has no place in him, for he dwelleth not in unholy temples. (Mosiah 2:29-37)

King Benjamin clearly defines the consequences of sin. Sin is rebellion against God. When one knows what is right and does wrong, he not only violates the law, but also puts himself in a state of opposition to God a serious offense in and of itself. If one doesn't *spiritually* understand the Word of Wisdom and the Law of Chastity, then one doesn't understand them at all! Following is a paraphrase of a story found in the *Book of Mormon Religion Student Manual* 121-122 about a bishop and a ward member.

A CUP OF COFFEE

A bishop tells the story of an elderly sister who came in for a temple recommend. When he asked her about adherence to the Word of Wisdom, she admitted that she had one cup of coffee each morning. He asked if she could quit and was told no, he suggested that he could not issue a recommend until compliance with the law was met. The woman grew very angry and said, "I don't think it is that significant! One cup of coffee is nothing. I can't believe a loving Father would hold me out of the celestial kingdom for one cup of coffee a day. Why, then, should you hold me out of the temple?" For a long moment the bishop looked at her and then said very gently, "I suppose that there are many, many things far more serious than a cup of coffee. Certainly one of those more serious things is rebellion against God. As a member of the Church you know what the Lord has taught concerning the Word of

Wisdom. If you know the law and still refuse to obey it, that is a very serious state of rebellion. So as long as you continue in this state of opposition you cannot dwell with God."

I often hear similar rational from *casual* LDS substance users. A teen might say to his parents "I can't believe you are so upset and angry because I smoked a little pot or looked at a couple of Playboys." As parents attempt to explain their concern in a "temporal" fashion, they typically suggest that marijuana and pornography will do something horrible to them. Such teachings mislead the user to expect these negative consequences to occur during the first stage of addiction. One must focus on the *spiritual* nature of substance misuse to teach God's commandments correctly.

SECOND STAGE OF ADDICTION

The second stage of addiction is depicted in the figure below.

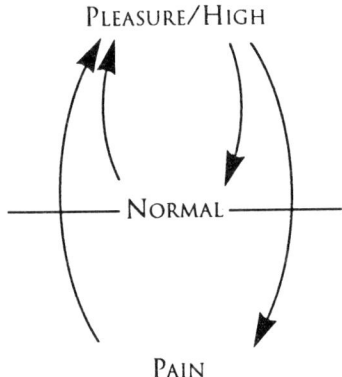

This stage is explained in 3 Nephi 27:11 "...*verily I say unto you they have joy in their works for a season and by and by the end cometh...*" During the second stage of addiction an "end cometh" to the pleasure, and pain is experienced periodically.

The scripture uses the word "season" to illustrate the variability of the time period between stages. A season in length varies around the world. A winter in Alaska is long and harsh; in Hawaii it is short and mild. Similarly, the period of time a person remains in the pleasure/joy stage of addiction also varies. Some individuals might remain in the pleasure/joy stage for many years. A "social drinker" is the type of individual who is able to remain in the first stage of the addiction for an extended time. On the other hand, a person might experience the pain, for example of becoming an alcoholic or a sex addict with the first drink or first exposure to pornography.

The second stage of addiction is one in which *tolerance* is developed. Tolerance occurs with drug and alcohol abuse, when over time it takes more of the same substance to get the same high. In other words, if one joint (marijuana cigarette) gets a person high during the first stage of addiction, the number of joints needed to get that same high will increase perhaps to five or six joints later in the addiction. A similar tolerance occurs with substances other than alcohol and drugs. For example, the principle of tolerance for pornography is noted by the LDS Church First Presidency in the pamphlet *For the Strength of Youth*. In the pamphlet we read:

> Pornography is especially dangerous and addictive. Curious exploration of pornography can become a controlling habit leading to coarser material and to sexual transgression. If you continue to view pornography, your spirit will become desensitized, and your conscience will erode. (LDS Church, 1990 p. 11, © Copyright by The Church of Jesus Christ of Latter-day Saints. Used by permission.)

As the amount of substance required to obtain the joy/high increases, so does the need to obtain the substance. That is, the time, money and energy needed to obtain enough of the substance to get the original high consumes more and more of the user's life. Stealing and other negative behaviors increase to support the habit. The small seed of disobedience that was planted during the first stage of addiction now begins to sprout.

It is in the middle stage of addiction that LDS substance users develop a marked change in moral values and behavior. Members of the LDS Church always compromise values as they progress into the middle stage of addiction. In many cases they do not forget their LDS values but simply develop another set of values referred to by many as "street values." For example, an LDS marijuana user may function regularly as a counselor in the Elder's Quorum presidency, he may go to the temple, and be very active in the church, and use marijuana only occasionally.

During the middle stages of addiction, the substance user continues to obtain periodic pleasure and joy and learns to cope with pain by using the effective and dependable substances. It is usually at this stage that surrounding loved ones first begin to suspect the misuse of substances.

WARNING SIGNS OF SUBSTANCE ABUSE

Characteristics of substance abuse typically become evident during the middle stages of addiction. The following groups of behaviors serve as warning symptoms of abuse:

CHANGES IN BEHAVIOR

- Chronic dishonesty [lying, stealing, cheating]; trouble with the police.
- Evasiveness when talking about friends and activities.
- Possession of large amounts of money.
- Increasing and inappropriate anger, hostility, irritability, and secretiveness.
- Reduced motivation, energy, self-discipline, and self-esteem.
- Diminished interest in extracurricular activities, church and hobbies.

IDENTIFICATION WITH A SUB-CULTURE

- Drug or sex-related magazines, slogans on clothing, and music.

- Conversation and joking that are preoccupied with alcohol, drugs, or immoral behavior.
- Hostility shown when alcohol, drugs, or morality are brought up for discussion.
- A new circle of friends also suspected of substance misuse.

DRAMATIC CHANGES IN SCHOOL AND WORK PERFORMANCE

- Marked downturn in grades-not just from C's to F's, but from A's to B's and C's.
- Assignments not completed.
- Increased absenteeism or tardiness at school or work.

OBVIOUS SIGNS OF SUBSTANCE MISUSE

- Possession of drug-related paraphernalia like pipes, rolling papers, small decongestant bottles, eye drops, and small butane torches.
- Possession or evidence of alcohol and drugs, such as pills, white powder, small glass vials, or hypodermic needles; peculiar plants, butts, seeds, or leaves in ashtrays or in clothing pockets; empty or hidden alcohol containers.
- Odor of drugs, smell of incense or other "cover-up" scents.
- Clear signs of intoxication, such as bloodshot eyes, slurred speech, inappropriate laughter.
- Possession of pornographic magazines, videos, or explicit sexual notes from friends.

MISCELLANEOUS SIGNS

Increased need for money.

As tolerance for a substance increases, the user requires *more* of it and must hustle the substance and the related lifestyle more actively. The user borrows from others; valuables disappear from the home;

earnings are spent without evidence of anything purchased; and legal charges for shoplifting may begin to occur. It should be noted that the increased need for money is not necessarily found in all cases. For example, females rarely have to pay with money for their drugs or alcohol if they attend parties or go to bars.

Spirituality decreases.
LDS substance users begin to rationalize and deny certain beliefs. They may become intolerant of religious discussions. Typically, they become less willing to attend various church activities. However, at times, LDS addicts will continue church attendance and maintain church assignments in an effort to hide their substance use and keep others "off their back." Nevertheless, a spiritual decline always occurs with the onset of addiction.

Lying in the LDS culture.
A special emphasis should be placed on the acceptance of lying in the LDS culture. Usually if a parent or another loved one confronts the substance user at this stage, the addict will likely deny or minimize use. Some substance users will deny any use with all the fervor, zest, and tears of a Book of Mormon testimony, even if clear signs of abuse are evident. At times the lying behavior extends all the way to priesthood leaders during priesthood interviews. It is important to realize that many of the characteristics seen at this stage of addiction are as much a part of the addiction as is the actual use of the substance itself. Any persistent changes in one's usual behavior are cause for concern and warrant further evaluation. Secrecy and deception walk hand in hand with the development of an addiction problem.

USING SUBSTANCE TO COPE WITH PAIN

As mentioned earlier, the substance user begins to experience some type of pain during the second stage of addiction. The pain includes discovery by police, parents, and peers. Among members of the LDS Church, an underlying guilt often develops as the user regularly uses substances and perhaps regularly goes to church. Other painful experiences include the consequences of poor judgment or illegal behavior associated with the substance use. Immorality and secretiveness are often found with substance use and increase the guilt experienced by the user. In this stage users have learned that substance use is an effective means of ridding themselves of the emotional pain and guilt, at least temporarily.

Third Stage of Addiction

The third and last stage of addiction begins as substance users experience more pain and are unable to reach the "highs" they were once able to achieve in the earlier stages of addiction. They are left with increasing levels of discomfort and pain. This stage is illustrated in the following figure.

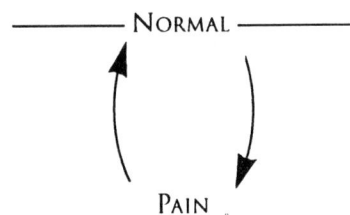

3 Nephi 27:11 continues as follows: "...*by and by the end cometh, and they are hewn down, and cast into the fire from whence there is no return.*" Elder Russell M. Nelson explained the progress of addiction ending in the third stage as follows:

> From an initial experiment thought to be trivial, a vicious cycle may follow. From trial comes a habit. From habit comes dependence. From dependence comes addiction. Its grasp is so gradual. Enslaving shackles of habit are too small to be sensed until they are too strong to be broken. Indeed, drugs are the modern "mess of pottage" for which souls are sold. No families are free from risk. (*Ensign* "Addiction or Freedom" November 1988 pp. 6-9. © Copyright by The Church of Jesus Christ of Latter-day Saints. Used by permission.)

Often the alcoholic or drug addict will switch drugs, mix drugs, or administer drugs in different ways in an attempt to regain the pleasure initially experienced. Sex addicts will do similarly by trying more risky sexual behavior in an effort to obtain the high experienced in the first stage of addiction. However, in the last stage of addiction the "season" or the "high" disappears, rarely to be found again.

Disease stage.
It is at this stage that the disease concept of addiction becomes evident. In order to understand the disease concept, examine the analogy of an epileptic using phenobarbital to prevent seizures. If an epileptic takes medication appropriately, he is free of seizures. If he forgets to take the medication for a long period of time, seizures return and pain is experienced. In a similar fashion, an addict, while taking marijuana, alcohol, or using pornography, perceives himself as normal and able to function at home, school, and work. However, if the substance is taken away, there could possibly be pain such as shakes, physical withdrawal, and emotional distress. Simply by using the substance again the addict perceives his condition as improved. A typical addict, while in this last stage of addiction, does not believe that he can function or even live without the substance.

The disease of addiction replaces free agency and spirituality. During this final stage of addiction, the small seed of disobedience planted earlier matures and blossoms. Here the user might more accurately be perceived as an "addict" or a "sick person needing to get well" and not as a "wicked person needing to repent."

To help one understand the addict's condition while in the third stage of addiction, visualize to what extent you might go to obtain air if your head were being held under water. Books, lectures, threats, promises, programs, and caring individuals likely make very little difference in causing you to change your desire for air. As long as your head is under water, you are in a life-threatening situation. This illustration might help you empathize with the desperation of the addict. The addict wants the substance, i.e. drugs, pornography, in the same way you would want air. The addict believes and feels that life cannot continue without the use of substances. Another way to view the last stage of addiction is by comparing it with a "spiritual death." Sin leads to misery, suffering and loss of agency for oneself.

UNIQUE LDS PROBLEMS

A personal experience with Satan.
Continuing with the analogy of being held under water, one might ask "Whose hand is holding one down?" If we return to The Word of Wisdom scriptures we can safely assume that the addict has fallen captive to Satan and his "evil conspiring men." One might wonder if the tremendous war in heaven for our free agency is not being continued here in earth life. If such is the case, Satan finally is able to capture what he was not able to obtain there-our free agency. Many LDS addicts have had experiences with Satan. Perhaps they were deeply involved with Satanism or perhaps only felt his presence. Nevertheless, it seems that because each has been baptized and given the gift of the Holy Ghost, Satan seems to knock stronger at their doors than perhaps he does at the doors of an non-LDS person.

Tell the "whole" story.
Many parents and leaders teach the reason not to break the Word of Wisdom or the Law of Chastity is all the horrible problems and pain that usually occur in the third stage of addiction. Unfortunately, many of our youth see their friends and even themselves in the first stage of addiction, just having a good time. Youth may suspect that those teaching them about addiction are lying, because most of their friends who misuse substances do not appear to have any problems. In fact,

those misusing alcohol, drugs or sex may be class officers, players on the football team, part of the popular crowd, or even steady church attenders. Thus, the only problem the youth see is the teacher's ignorance about addiction. Such a perception often increases the LDS youth's curiosity and risk for the future misuse of substances.

Healthy vs. Unhealthy Addictions.
Certainly there are numerous addictions that are healthy. Those individuals who take medications as prescribed by a doctor could be considered as having a healthy addiction. Medications for high blood pressure, seizures, and mental illness help chemically imbalanced individuals to be become more normal in their functioning. (Refer to diagram depicting the third and final stage of addiction.) Healthy addictions not only allow the individual to function normally, they may increase an individual's ability to grow and become more spiritual. On the other hand, unhealthy addictions always end in spiritual decay, with *dishonesty* as a symptom. So be mindful that in the case of prescription medication, the same drug and same frequency of use may have a different effect on two separate individuals. For one it might be a healthy addiction which allows the individual to be more normal and to grow spiritually. For the other, the drug use might lead to spiritual ruin.

A FINAL NOTE

An individual from a healthy LDS family might reach the last stage of an addiction by first using the substance out of curiosity. This is because the can of Coors Light or the Playboy centerfold does not ask the addict's permission or religious affiliation before the "seasons" of addiction evolve.

Age has nothing to do with an individual's progression through the disease stage of addiction. A nine-year-old or 99-year-old might progress through the various stages of addiction. Many prospective missionaries share their intentions to use substances "only for awhile" and then "clean up" to go on their missions. For those able to remain in the first stage of addiction, such *is* the outcome. However, for the many less fortunate ones who proceed further into the addiction stages, free agency is lost and a mission is *no* longer a choice for them. Addicts are cut off from their family, siblings, and God because of their disobedience to a previous religious commitment.

Elder Boyd K. Packer summarized the addiction cycle in an LDS General Conference address. He said:

> ...*Then many of them turn elsewhere, seeking to escape the futility in life. They turn to drugs and find for a moment the escape they seek. At last their spirits soar. They reach beyond themselves, erase all limitations, and taste for a moment, as they suppose, that which they have been seeking. But it is a synthetic, a wicked counterfeit, for they return to a depression worse than the one they left. Then they become players in the saddest of human tragedies. For, as they turn again to this release, they are not seeking what they sought before, but indulge to escape the consequences of each previous adventure with drugs. This is addiction! This is slavery! When a remedy becomes worse than the disease, then we have found futility itself...*(General Conference, "Escape From Futility", Oct. 3, 1969. © Copyright by The Church of Jesus Christ of Latter-day Saints. Used by permission.)

RECOVERY STAGE

One might ask, "How do addicts recover if they have lost their free agency to Satan and their willpower has become ineffective?" The answer is obvious and simple. The main problem with breaking a temporal commandment like the Word of Wisdom is the decline of spirituality, so, it follows that the main resource in recovery is the increase of spirituality. God our Heavenly Father is more powerful than Satan and his forces. Unless the addict obtains a moment of clarity in which a higher power intervenes and a miracle occurs, there will be no recovery from the last stage of addiction. Only God can return the addict's agency to freely choose "not" to use. Unlike many regular church-going LDS members who can function quite well without reading the scriptures, without having their prayers answered, and without a personal relationship with a higher power, an addict will not be freed from Satan's grasp of addiction unless divine intervention occurs.

Even non-LDS persons recognize the importance of spirituality in recovery. Alcoholics Anonymous (A.A.) is credited worldwide for having successfully helped numerous alcoholics recover from addiction. Interestingly, A.A. concedes a "higher power" and a "spiritual program" as key ingredients in obtaining sobriety. Treatment programs don't cure; only the power of God can break Satan's chains of bondage.

The following poem illustrates the point. The poem was shared with me by Marc L. an LDS addict six years into recovery.

> Humpty Dumpty sat on a wall.
> Humpty Dumpty had a great fall.
> All the King's horses,
> And all the King's men
> Couldn't put Humpty together again.
> But, the King could.

CHAPTER TWO

HI, I'M TONY AND I'M AN ALCOHOLIC
(A Personal Story of Addiction)

I guess I've never thought more about a statement in my life, and humbly say today, "My name is Tony and I'm an alcoholic." Maybe I can start with just a little bit of my story to let you know where I've come from and what we have felt in our home through tragedy as well as the return of the Spirit of Christ. I was born in to one of the most fun homes that anyone could wish for. My dad was gone quite a bit, doing church work and trying to make a living as a young father. My mom was very fun loving. They did the very best job of parenting they could. I thought they were great. I want you to know that if I could have chosen any home, it would have been the home I was raised in. If I could have chosen to change anything about my father and mother, there would have been only one thing-to have more time with them. I really have no complaints. Because my father is so high in the Church, some therapists I'd see would want to find some fault with him. I guess his only fault was that he loved me too much. He thought I was the greatest and wanted me to have every advantage.

I remember that many things came natural for me. I was a pretty good athlete. I had friends. I didn't care about school, whether that was natural or not. Everything was going along just fine. If you had asked me about life going into my senior year, I'd have said I had a dream come true. I was playing varsity basketball and had professional baseball contract offers. I thought I had everything.

Then I did what a noble LDS boy would do; I went on a mission. My mission again was a dream come true. My mission president happened to be a general authority. I was called to be an assistant when I was out eleven months. I enjoyed my mission and converting nonmembers to the gospel of Jesus Christ. Of all the thrills I had in athletics (like being carried off the court, making the last shot, or sitting in front of a scout who was trying to get me to play pro ball), the greatest thrill I ever had was watching a young family walk into the waters of baptism. I guess I felt as close to the Lord as anyone could have felt. It was a time in my life when I knelt down and asked direct questions and I got direct answers. You could have held a gun to my head and said, "Deny that there is a God or that the LDS Church is not His church." I could not have denied any of it to save my own or anyone else's life. I just knew the truth.

I came home, fell in love and got married. My wife and I really had a fun first four years. I guess the tragedy of our lives was when the doctors said we wouldn't be able to have any children. Under those circumstances, the Lord made up for it. He called me to be the Young Men's president for nine years. So I had all the sons a guy would ever want, and I loved them.

One year, on the day after Thanksgiving, a close friend and I were taking these boys out goose hunting. Suddenly, a couple of drunks crossed over the center line and hit us head on. My friend hit the steering wheel, his heart exploded, and he died. I was sitting between the two seats and the back seat broke off with two of the boys in it hitting me in the back and breaking it into three places. The engine came up and broke my pelvis, and then I went through the windshield. The next thing I remember was waking up and seeing a television set above my head that told whether I was alive or not. I heard the doctor say I had a forty percent chance to live and no chance at all to walk again.

I looked over and they had a bottle of Demerol dripping into my arm. When I felt that Demerol my entire life changed. I was on a Demerol drip for a month and a half. It started when I was unconscious. I am a genetic, sociological, emotional, alcoholic, drug addict. There was a dream come true for me in my arm. All the feelings of not being good enough, of failure, of every problem that I had ever heaped on myself, were better, because of what was dripping into my arm. I felt a cure for all the pain I had created in my heart.

I've gained a new understanding about "anonymity" in my life. It is not that you shouldn't go out and say that "Tony F." is an "alcoholic." That's only part of it. Anonymity is when I walk into the detox center, or into the gutter with another alcoholic or addict, and I am just "Tony, an alcoholic." All the money in the bank, my family (whom I came close to losing) didn't matter. I am an alcoholic. In 12-step recovery programs such as A.A. and S.A.V.E., we are all the same. We are simply children of God struggling with a disease.

Let me tell you a little about my drug use. I don't think I ever took a drug legally. If the doctor said one was good, four were better. My doctor had done some questionable things. He might have thought I was going to sue him. So he gave me almost an unlimited supply of Percodan #5 and Valium #10. I took these like candy. I honestly think if I took them now it would be a lethal dose. I was taking five Percodan #5 and five #10 Valiums at one time. People attempt suicide on less than that. I remember the night they had changed drug types on me, and I can tell you what it was like watching the death angel stand at the door and wait. That I was going to die a drug addict was one of the most terrifying things in my life. The Lord eventually blessed my wife and I with children. Not to have a chance to hold these little ones, or to watch them grow up, all my dreams and hopes dying in a bottle.

I watched my wife become a codependent. My dad came to her and said, "I think Tony's an addict and needs help." She said, "Mind your own business." I loved her even more. I loved her for those statements. What a kind codependent. I would feel like going somewhere and she would say, "You just stay here. Do you need any pills?" I'd say, "I don't think those three are working. I'd better get a couple of more." I'd crack my back and learn how to move just right to get sympathy. I learned how to use people for my gain. The only gain I wanted was my drugs this was my goal in life; everything else centered around it, not around four little children who needed a father, or a wife who needed a husband, or a church who needed a member, or my parents who wanted a son. It was just me and feeding that craving.

My doctor was killed in a plane crash and, instantly, my source dried up. I'll never forget the pain of going through withdrawal. One day I was driving along the road in my car and I saw a liquor store. It had been ten years since I had tried alcohol. I'd drunk about five times while in high school. I thought maybe alcohol would help get me through the jitters of the drug withdrawal. At that point I crawled into a bottle. I drank for five years without anyone knowing-I was a closet drinker. I didn't go to bars. Can I tell you of the loneliness I experienced? Can I tell you what it's like to stand in a garage late at night with a cup in your hand, shaking, with tears streaming down your cheeks, and saying, "Please, dear God, don't let me. Please stop me. I know you're there. I think you still love me. But please stop me." But I couldn't stop because I have a disease. The cravings were more than I could bear. I would stop for a little while but the pain in my heart would be too much. When I was able to stay sober for a while, I'd start thinking, "Now I have to be successful." "Now I really have to be a father." "Now I have to really be an intimate, loving, gentle husband." Then all the fears would come back and into the bottle I'd go. Under these conditions working in the church was very difficult for me. I guess if I could have run and hidden from any name, "hypocrite" would have been number one. I felt like the greatest hypocrite that had ever walked on the planet. My father is a General Authority. He claimed I was a "chip off the old block," and he frequently said, "He is going to be like me. He loves the Church and loves the Lord." After five years of drinking, one day when I was drunk and driving home, the police pulled me over. My tolerance level for alcohol was unbelievable. I thought I was driving just fine. The police said I had a blood alcohol level of .385, but I wasn't as drunk as usual, and my family didn't know.

There was no way to hide my drinking now. The police called my wife. I remember being out gardening when my dad came down to help plant flowers at our new house. I stood there and thought, "I have to tell him myself." I told him I'd never let him be fooled by anything. At least this way he could say he knew. I said "Dad, I got a DUI." I know his father's history, that he died of alcoholism, that he was a mean, ugly alcoholic. (I was a sleepy one. I thought that was better.) You could have taken a baseball bat to my father and it wouldn't have hurt him as bad as those words did from me. From that moment on, I admitted to myself that I was an alcoholic. There wasn't a day that went by that I didn't try to stop drinking. Not a day that would go by that I wouldn't promise myself to stop tomorrow. I still wanted to be what I could be as a father and Church member. I didn't want to tell the bishop and stake president and be released. I loved what I was doing in church service.

Under those conditions, I continued along a path of incredible mental and emotional turmoil. I experienced feelings of guilt and shame. Guilt is; "I made a mistake." Shame is; "I am a mistake." I felt them both. I made a mistake, but I'm not good enough anyway. The other rationalization I kept using was the excuse that my father holds the apostolic priesthood. "He'll give me a blessing and God will take this from me," I told myself. I really believed that something would happen that would kick me out of this incredible craving. I lived with the emotional pain that I was a hypocrite, a liar, a cheat, and a stealer- everything I despised in life, I was. I was telling everyone else they shouldn't be doing this or that, and then I'd sneak out to my car for a drink. I'd rather have died than have been an alcoholic.

I finally went into treatment, but I went to a place where no one would know me. I tried to use a fake name but they wouldn't let me. That showed a lot of progress, didn't it? In fact, my early recovery was as bad as my alcoholism. To tell the truth, the first few A.A. meetings I went to were "Gay Alcoholics Anonymous" meetings. I didn't know any alcoholics or gays, so I thought I'd be safe there. Who could I run into? Yet, I'd go to these meetings, sit in my car, and watch every person who went in. If I recognized someone, I'd find another meeting.

Later while I was in the county detox center I admitted that I was powerless over alcohol and that my life had become unmanageable. Eight years later, I'm still trying to get it in my heart, eight years of staggering because I did too much in my head and not enough in my heart. Sure I could see the DUIs. I could see all these things piling up, but I didn't feel the pain.

Let me tell you of the intervention that happened to me. I went to county detox. I was there with every race, creed, and color, what I would have called "low life," and I belonged there. I was no better than any one. They had lice and even worse diseases. Three of the bigger guys decided they were going to rape me. This is the best intervention ever done to me or that I have heard of. I called my wife and said,"You need to get me out of here. There are three big guys who want to rape me." She said, "Maybe it is better to get raped than drunk." That would put you back a step or two, wouldn't it? I said to her again, "No, I don't think you understand-not snuggle with me, they want to rape me." But that's how my intervention happened. For she, who had never violated a code had come to the understanding that it was better that I was raped than to drink again.

The other intervention was God's doing. I was still in county detox and I was about to enter a treatment program because I couldn't do it on my own. I have as much will power as anyone, and I'm telling you I couldn't do it alone. I called my wife the night before I was going into the center. I said, "Please come and get me. I want to spend one more night with the kids before I go in for 30 days treatment." She said, "Let me think about it and I'll call you back in a half hour." I went to the back of county detox and shut the bathroom door. I knelt down next to a toilet and with all the humility I could raise, I said, "I'm willing to do anything you say God. I'm willing to go into treatment for 30 days. I will do it if you will let me go home." I continued, "If you will let me go home again to spend one night with my children, if you'll let me have just one chance to lay on the bed and hold those four little ones in my arms and tell them I love them, I will do anything you say."

An hour passed with no phone call. An hour and a half passed and then two hours. I called her back. She said, "I'm not going to come." I remember hanging up the phone. I went back and lay on the bed. In this massive room full of bodies, I thought, "Why?" The second intervention came when God said, "You have it wrong, my son. When you are willing to do anything I say you will have them for eternity, not just one night."

Let me tell you what my recovery program means to me. I thought I could do everything alone. I didn't pray to God; I checked in. I would just kneel down and say, "Thanks for this and that. We're having a great time. Let the show begin." That was basically my prayer. I can't do that anymore. My prayers now are simple. I say, "Please dear God, help me stay sober, today. Please dear God, help my children and wife find serenity. In the name of Jesus Christ, Amen." I love the twelve steps of A.A. and S.A.V.E. You know the A.A. concept that saves me is "maintaining a conscious contact with my higher power." I don't have any choice. When I'm driving down the road I have to think, "Heavenly Father what should I do? Thanks just for being here. I just need a friend. I just need to know that I'm your son and you care about me." I guess my sweetest meetings are by myself. There was a change for me. The *Book of Mormon* calls it a "change of heart." I no longer have desire to do evil.

It is not that we stopped using or drinking that is the secret to recovery. The giant genius, the grandness of recovery is that we admitted that *alone* we couldn't, but that we had the courage, the strength and the faith, to say with God's help we can do it. Then we were willing to take other steps. These are not fun. They include doing a searching and fearless moral inventory of our lives. This step frightened me above all. To admit what I really was, that I am not a General Authority's son or an elder's quorum president I'm Tony. I'm an individual. I have all the possibilities and capabilities without anyone else. I am God's son. That leaves me with infinite possibilities, hope, humility, and love.

If God had given me the choice of a disease, to have an addiction would not have been my first choice. But if He had given me the choice of a recovery people, people working a twelve-step program would be the choice. If I could have chosen a recovery church the LDS church would be it. If I could have chosen a family, my family is the one I would have chosen. As I said at the start, "I'm Tony. I'm an alcoholic." To me it is a statement of conviction. Not that I haven't made mistakes, but I've resolved that my family need not go through the problems of dysfunction anymore. The miracle in our lives is that dysfunction doesn't have to go any further. It can stop because of the atonement of Christ, because of loving fellowships and friendships. Because we are there for one another, it need not go on.

I guess my prayer for all of us is no longer to desire that *our* will be done, but His. No longer to think we have to control others or their problems, but to do His will. As the Savior said, "Not my will but thine be done."

CHAPTER THREE

THE LDS FAMILY
ADJUSTING TO ADDICTION

A rather widely accepted notion is that when addiction strikes a family, the surrounding loved ones experience distress as well as the addict. Elder David B. Haight, addressing a United States Senate Sub-Committee Hearing (in June 1977) on behalf of The Church Of Jesus Christ of Latter-day Saints, announced, "...Conservatively estimating each problem drinker [drug abuser] has a direct impact on the lives of at least four other persons...." The LDS Church provides a manual for such families which acknowledges the impact of addiction on the family and includes a unit entitled "The Effects of Alcohol on the Family." The purpose of that unit is

> ...to help each family member better understand the destructive process that takes place within a family when one or more of its members has a drinking problem." (*Resource Manual for Helping Families with Alcohol Problems* p. 41. © Copyright by The Church of Jesus Christ of Latter-day Saints. Used by permission.)

A normal healthy family (and even families not so normal and healthy) typically adjust to the disease of addiction by developing characteristic behaviors.

The aim of this chapter is to describe these adaptive behaviors. Most professionals label this adaptive process as codependency. The term "codependent" is used because those behaviors exhibited by surrounding loved ones often *depends* upon what the addict might or might not do. Codependent behaviors that develop among surrounding loved ones are similar across substances. To explain, those codependent problems experienced by the spouse of a sex addict would be similar to those problems of a spouse of an alcoholic.

Codependent behaviors exhibited by surrounding loved ones can be categorized into three groups, which are: Rescuing Behaviors, Persecuting Behaviors, and Suffering Behaviors. Additionally, it seems that LDS families adapt somewhat differently than non-LDS families to the addiction process. These adaptive characteristics occur innocently and slowly over time. The manner in which behaviors of an addict codepend on the behaviors of surrounding loved ones is depicted in the diagram below.

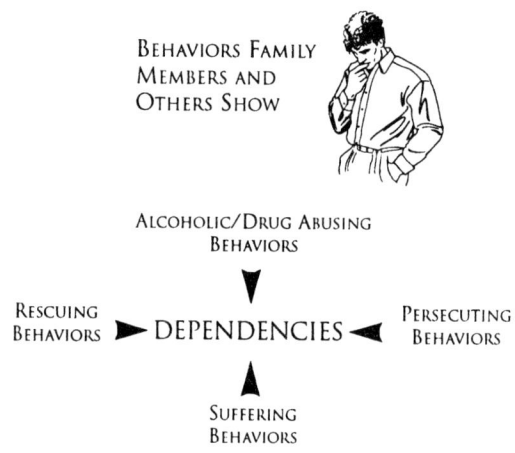

It is important to note that codependent behaviors are not "right" or "wrong," but are simply how a typical family adjusts to the addiction process. In addition, not all surrounding loved ones will experience all the codependent behaviors, nor will they necessarily progress through the various phases of codependency in the same order.

Many treatment programs use labels such as "Victim," "Martyr," "Persecutor," "Enabler," and "Co-alcoholic" to describe codependents. However, rather than using these labels, the term "behaviors" will be used in this discussion to refer to the family's distress. Each of us is a child of God, who has developed certain behaviors in an effort to cope with the addict. These behaviors, like other behaviors, can be changed with God's help.

The family typically adjusts to the disease of addiction as illustrated on the chart entitled "The LDS Family Adjusting to Addiction" located at the end of this chapter. If family members can recognize these behavior patterns, they will understand more clearly what is happening and make better plans to help themselves and the addict. With that thought in mind, take a closer look at some of these behavior patterns.

RESCUING BEHAVIORS

It is impossible for addicts in the last stages of addiction to be responsible. Therefore, someone must help them fulfill their responsibilities. *Behind every irresponsible substance abuser is a hyper-responsible parent or spouse.* They are often the first behaviors developed by surrounding loved ones. Rescuing behaviors save substance abusers from the immediate consequences of their own substance use. These behaviors include denying, lying, and covering-up.

DENYING

Denial is a common behavior developed by surrounding loved ones of an addict. Several assumptions follow someone who admits that a member of his or her family has a problem with substances. One assumption is the false believe that "if there is a problem with them then there must be a problem with me." In essence, you assume *you* have failed because *they* have a problem. If it is your child, then you have failed as a parent. If it is your spouse, then you have failed as a partner. If it is your parent, then you have failed as a child. Much pain, guilt, and confusion come with accepting the truth that a loved one has a substance abuse problem.

The intensity of denial seems greater with those who are sincerely involved in religious practice. The more active a person in Church, the more a person strives to do what he feels is right, such as holding family home evenings and attending church, the more difficult it will be for him to work through denial. The Church's manual on alcohol problems states:

> Denial is the most serious problem that the...family has to overcome before they can begin to help themselves. (*Resource Manual for Helping Families with Alcohol Problems* p. 5. © Copyright by The Church of Jesus Christ of Latter-day Saints. Used by permission.)

Members of the LDS Church tend to be so fearful that substance abuse will happen that they deny and overlook the clear signs of it. An analogy that helps explain the concept of denial is that of a child who recently went swimming. If that child were standing dripping wet by the swimming pool, wearing a swimming suit, we would not likely ask questions like "Where have you been?" "What have you been doing?" Codependents however, *often* confront addicts when they come home two hours late, with bloodshot eyes, glassy stares, and a strange odor-by asking, "Where have you been?" "What have you been doing?" Perhaps the Golden Question most commonly asked by LDS codependents when alcohol, drugs or paraphernalia are found is "Whose is this?" The substance abuser's Golden Answer is "I'm holding it for a friend." We want to believe their responses, so we continue to rescue them from the consequences of their behavior by denying the obvious and accepting their lies. Often it takes the equivalent of a Grand Jury conviction for LDS families to admit that a loved one has a substance abuse problem.

INCREASED RELIGIOUS ACTIVITES

Religious activities often increase during the first stage of codependency. The codependent firmly believes that fasting, prayer, and careful obedience to each of God's commandment will cure the addict. Loved ones often commit to reading the scriptures, going to the church, and having family home evening more regularly. The underlying goal for such behavior appears to be: "Get God to fix the addict."

COVERING-UP

Covering up is a specific behavior that codependents exhibit to clean up or make things better after the addict has been irresponsible. For example, a wife might call her spouse's work to report him "ill" with the flu when, in reality, he is in bed with a hangover. In an effort to save their child from a police record and horrible experiences in lock-up parents of an addict will run to the police station to rescue their child. A codependent will clean up the broken glass or hide the empty beer cans, even miss important church meetings in order to perform the necessary cover-up behaviors.

A codependent frequently seeks financial assistance by working part time or soliciting financial help from family or church authorities or both, in an effort to cover up the financial problems caused by the addict's habits. A codependent often becomes so effective in covering up the consequences of the substance abuse problem that even the addict might very truthfully say, "There's no problem." In other words, even the addict does not realize the problems that he or she might be causing, because the codependent has done such a thorough job in covering up.

LYING

Rescuing behaviors become so intense that codependents will begin to tell "white lies," saying that "It's not that bad" or "I'm fine" or "Its Okay," when confronted by the bishop, home teacher or close friends. In reality, a codependent may have just found a stack of pornographic magazines and a few pornographic videos. This lying process is called "minimization" and it is a rescuing behavior. The lies are typically unintentional and often unnoticed. They are shared with children, neighbors, church leaders and, sadly, with self.

PERSECUTING BEHAVIORS

Persecuting behaviors comprise the second stage or group of behaviors typically experienced by those close to an addict. Elder Marvin J. Ashton of the Council of the Twelve is among the many who have experienced the sad effects of substance abuse. A news article entitled, "Today, I am angry," states the following:

> I have just returned from a visit to the St. Marks Hospital in the Salt Lake Valley. Time was spent with an 82-year-old poor widow who had been beaten during the night by a grandson. Her skull was fractured, her right ear was torn so badly plastic surgery was required, her head was so heavily bandaged, I could hardly see her face. The nurse indicated her entire body was aching from pain.
>
> Apparently her grandson had been on drugs most of the day and had gone to her humble apartment to get money to purchase more. When she did not cooperate financially, he physically abused her and fled. ("Church News," *Deseret News*, Week Ending December 26, 1987 p. 14. © Copyright by The Church of Jesus Christ of Latter-day Saints. Used by permission.)

In this news article the addict appears to be in the third or disease stage of addiction. Elder Ashton momentarily experiences anger because of the addict's violent behavior toward the elderly woman. Anger is the source for most persecuting behaviors. Loved ones become angry because of the abuser's harmful or embarrassing actions. These can lead to great resentment by the addict's family and friends. Persecuting behaviors include nagging, threatening, and blaming. These behaviors become the source of persecution for the substance abuser in attempts by the codependent to control. Unfortunately, the very conservative LDS teachings that instruct the members of the church *not* to use drugs or pornography tend to set the stage for the development of persecuting behaviors. That is, these teachings translate to harsh opinions, labeling, and misunderstandings.

RELIGIOUS ACTIVITIES DECREASE

Increased religious behaviors which are tried by codependents as a rescuing behavior fail. Reality sets in because the addict has continued to abuse substances regardless of the codependent's religious pursuits. The codependent feels that the prayer, fasting, and other religious activities attempted as rescuing behaviors were unsuccessful. The codependent, out of despair, turns away from God to his or her own personal power, returning to the previous level of religious activity. This seems to occur because "God didn't solve" the problem.

THREATS

The codependent becomes desperate because all of the attempts to control or fix the addict seem to have failed. He or she may exhibit a variety of threats during this stage of codependence. These threats are usually extreme in nature. In the case of a spouse, divorce and separation are suggested. Often in the LDS family, threats take the form of laying guilt or shame in an attempt to force the addict into sobriety. Such threats are unsuccessful because of their extreme nature, and they are seldom implemented.

IRRATIONAL BEHAVIORS

As the addiction progresses, codependents become increasingly desperate and reach a point where they will try almost anything to control the addiction problem. One active member of the Church placed honey in her husband's bedding when he continually came home with pornographic magazines. The wife stated, "I could no longer keep my anger in. I wanted him to feel as miserable as I did." Numerous examples of irrational codependent behavior exist.

SUFFERING BEHAVIORS

Suffering behaviors make up the third stage of codependence. The persecuting and rescuing behaviors have failed to cure the addict. Elder John K. Carmack, member of the First Quorum of the Seventy, grew up with a brother who was an alcoholic. He recalls part of his story in a pamphlet published by S.A.V.E.

> I didn't realize it then, but looking back now he was probably drinking during those times. He was an alcoholic by the time he was 12 or 13. Most of the time we had a very loving and good relationship. When we lived in Santa Barbara, he seemed to always be away from home. Mother would spend her nights trying to find him. I believe that my mother went prematurely gray trying to handle this son. (*By The Things Which They Suffer*, S.A.V.E., 1987)

George P. Lee a former member of the First Quorum of the Seventy and of the LDS Church, also grew up where alcoholism was prevalent. He stated,

> I was witness to the day my three younger brothers began drinking. They were very young then. Not long after this, one of them had too much to drink one cold day. He wandered away from our hogan and never returned. Lonely and helpless, he stumbled around and lost his way in the bitter cold night. The next day he was found frozen. He was just sixteen. How I loved him. How deeply this pierced my soul is beyond what words can describe. I had taken care of him when he was but an infant. I had changed his diapers, fed him, wiped away his tears, and

held him. A part of me passed away too. (*Like Enos of Old*, S.A.V.E., 1987)

These Elders' stories illustrate the distress, worry, and suffering often experienced by loved ones of an addict. These behaviors are shown by people who suffer the consequences of the substance abuser's irresponsible actions. Examples of suffering include guilt, feelings of inadequacy, and shame.

GUILT

Typically codependents ask themselves what they might have done to cause the substance abuse problem and how they might have prevented it. They might ask themselves, "What did we do wrong?" Often they review every detail of the addict's life. Many families who seek counsel report regular family prayer, regular family home evening, and magnification of Church callings, and they still have an addict in their home. They conclude, "We must have failed somewhere." In a codependent's thinking, one plus one is supposed to equal two. If there is an addiction problem, there must be a parent or spouse problem. As a result, codependents feel guilty regardless of whether they find reasonable fault or not.

In some cases, surrounding loved ones may have indeed made some serious mistakes, particularly those who may have been abusive to their child, either physically or emotionally. Such behaviors certainly can predispose a person to substance abuse. Often at this stage the codependent feels unworthy to maintain a church calling, attend the temple, or even call upon God. They believe they are being justly punished for their sins by having a loved one suffer from addiction. Codependents who are Mormons carry not only society's "oughts and shoulds," they also add the "oughts and shoulds" of their religion to their already oppressive load. Instead of helping the codependent overcome his oppression, their wrong perspective of Christ and of the gospel suppresses them even further. Instead of *grace* they experience *guilt*.

DEPRESSION AND DEFEAT

The end result of suffering behaviors is defeat. Nothing has worked. Prescription drug use and counseling might have been sought by the codependent to deal with the addict. Withdrawal from social activities, excessive worrying, and possible physical ailments begin to occur. Occasional thoughts of death may also exist. One good sister recalled of this stage, "I didn't want to kill myself, but I often wished that my car might hit a telephone pole or something." Codependents acknowledge their powerlessness over their own lives and that of the addict. They experience in a personal way what Christ taught in Matthew 10:36: "And a man's foes [enemies] shall be they of his own household."

LOSS OF PERSONAL FREEDOM

Juel G., a codependent, explains that codependency is "when you feel responsible for how the addict acts or feels." He goes on to say, "Eventually you are led into bondage." As you assume responsibility for the addict's acts or feelings, the following occurs:

1. You become subject to manipulation or control by the addict.
2. You eliminate yourself as a resource to the addict.
3. You tend to rescue the addict.
4. Your self-esteem goes down.
5. You become depressed and experience mood swings based on the addict's behaviors.
6. You interfere with God's great gift of Free Agency and the Law of Justice.
7. You are *not* free to act for yourself!

As a codependent becomes entangled in the addict's web of needs, freedom is lost. President Marion C. Romney states:

> Man cannot be an agent unto himself unless he is self-reliant. Independence and self-reliance are critical factors in our spiritual growth.

Whenever our self-reliance is threatened, our freedom is threatened as well. *The more dependent we become, the less freedom we have to act.* (*Melchizedek Priesthood Personal Study Guide* 1989, p. 107, *emphasis added*. © Copyright by The Church of Jesus Christ of Latter-day Saints. Used by permission.)

As codependents come to understand the powerful dynamics of codependence, they will begin to see how their good intentions and forced solutions produce few positive results, and usually enable the addict to rationalize and continue using substances. Codependents believe they are cut off from God through embarrassment, deprivation, shame, pride, grief, and other feelings that emerge as symptoms of codependence.

Family and friends become codependent as their feelings and actions increasingly depend on what the substance abuser does or doesn't do. Gradually, codependents lose control over their own emotions and behavior and they deal with the substance abuser by adapting and exhibiting the behaviors of rescuing, persecuting and suffering. *Codependency is at its strongest when loved ones become so preoccupied and worried about working out the salvation of the addict that their own salvation is neglected and jeopardized.* In the end everyone becomes his or her own problem. Codependents can learn to become responsible *to* each other, instead of responsible *for* each other. Eventually, the codependent can acknowledge that they didn't *cause* the addiction, they can't *cure* the addiction, and that they can't *control* the addiction. This acknowledgement is accomplished by the codependent learning how to love the addict as God loves him.

The LDS Family Adjusting To Addiction

CODEPENDENCY

Rescuing Behaviors

Denial
Takes Responsibilities
Problems Multiply
Lying

Suspicion
Blues
Irritability
Covering-up
Religious Activities Increase

Persecuting Behaviors

Threats
Anger
Seeks Help

Problems Increase
Religious "Sermons"
Irrational Behaviors
Religious Activities Decrease

Suffering Behaviors

Quits Church Job
Depression
Self-Neglect
Spiritual Numbing
Thoughts of Death

Feelings of Unworthiness
Excessive Worry
Guilt and Shame
Admits Defeat

Bottom

Chapter Four

Without Love

By Vaughn J. Featherstone

I'd like to share some very personal experiences that convey a message of hope to those of you who may be experiencing the trauma of alcohol of drug abuse in your homes. I know from first-hand experience what a life of misery alcohol can cause.

I believe that my dad was probably an alcoholic before he and my mother were married. At that time, my mother was partial to the Catholic Church though not a member. Dad was a member of the Mormon Church, but he wasn't active. The children just came along one right after another, and soon there were eight of us in the family. As we grew up, we moved into the Salt Lake City area and started going to the Mormon Church just because it was handy and we had asked if we could go.

My dad was a steam shovel operator. In those days, during the Depression, when $15 to $20 a week. was a good wage, my dad was making $100 a week. But we didn't see it. He would get drunk every payday, and we wouldn't see him again until all his money was gone.

I remember one particular Wednesday night when my mother waited at the mantel, as she did every payday. She looked up the street where the bus would go by. I know that in her heart was a prayer that dad would get off the bus. But he never did. That night, there was no food in the house, and we went to bed hungry. About 10:30 that night, when I went to bed, my mother was still looking out the window over the mantel, and when I got up the next morning, she was still standing there looking out the window. I don't know if she stood there all night. I just kind of think maybe she did. I think her heart was too heavy for her to rest.

As I went into the living room she came up to me, handed me a list and asked, "Would you take this up to Mr. Parson's store and ask him if we can charge these groceries?" I remember saying to her, "Why do I always have to do it? Can't you get one of the other kids to do it? I hate to beg for groceries!" Then, I saw a terrible hurt look on her face and I told her, "I'll go." I remember going out and getting our old red wagon with the rims worn flat. I dragged it as slowly as a human being can walk, up the street to Mr. Parson's store. I got to the store, went in and walked around the aisles trying to avoid Mr. Parsons, who by the way was a high priest in our ward, though I didn't know at that time. Finally I walked up to him and handed him the note. He read it: "Dear Mr. Parsons, We don't have any food in the house and my children are hungry. Would you mind charging fifty pounds of flour, a bucket of lard, some side pork, and a few other things? We promise to pay back every penny when we get some money. Thanks Mrs. Featherstone."

I saw that great high priest and store owner look at the letter, then down at me, and tears came to his eyes. He got a big grocery cart, and then he pushed it around the store and filled it up with all those things. He made out a charge slip and put it in the wagon, and I dragged it home. I did that more times than I can tell you. I was embarrassed, bitterly embarrassed, every single time. I give the credit to my mother and older brothers that we paid back every single penny that we ever borrowed from Mr. Parsons and from another grocer who gave us a charge account.

At about the same time in my life, we couldn't afford much clothing, either. I had a pair of shoes that I'd wear to church. They weren't the best shoes. They had holes in the soles, so I cut out pieces of cardboard and slid them inside my shoes. When I sat in church, I kept both feet flat on the floor. I didn't want anyone to see some kind of advertisement, like *Quaker Oats*, across the bottom. Another Sunday, I noticed the tops of my shoes were also gone. So, I went to a box of shoes our neighbors had given us and only one pair fit me. They were a pair of women's white nursing shoes with high heels. I remember being in my Sunday School class downstairs, and the teacher had us sit in a big half-circle so we were all on the front row. I will never forget how I felt. Each on of my shoes felt two feet in diameter. I just sat there the whole time watching everyone in class to see if they would look at my shoes. I knew if anyone laughed at me, I could never go back to church again. It would be too much for a nine-year-old to handle. I remember sitting and watching everybody's eyes.

My family once was down on Second South between West Temple and Main Street. In those days this was not a good part of town. I was just a baby in my mother's arms. Ronald, my older brother, was about one-and-a-half years old and my oldest brother was just under three. My dad was drinking in a bar. We sat and sat in the car waiting, and he wouldn't come out. It was snowing at the time. It had snowed four or five inches. That wonderful mother of mine put me in one arm and my brother in the other arm and we walked home. I saw my mother hurt as much as any mother can hurt and struggle and try to hold things together with seven little children. One died of phenomena because of problems incidental to exposure.

I saw this great woman put on logger boots and men's clothing and go out to work at Garfield's Smelter. She would pick up the bus at about 10 p.m. and work from 11 p.m. to 7:00 a.m. She would get home by 8 a.m. or so and wake all the kids up and get us off to school. I don't know when she slept or got the washing done. She would fix our meals and come home for lunch. I simply couldn't add one particle of burden to her heart.

While I was growing up, we didn't have prayer in my home. I would go out alone at night, stand on the front porch, look up and not know what to say. I had never been taught how to pray, so I memorized the Lord's Prayer. I often wondered if my prayer would get through, so I'd pray again. Then I would finally feel like maybe God heard me. Sometimes, I would go out into the backyard, kneel down behind the bushes, and offer a prayer because I felt terribly embarrassed to pray in my home.

Outside of the home, Dad was terrific to everybody else's kids. He was kind to them and they thought he was great. But when he came home, he would be different. If we let the rabbits go hungry or didn't happen to feed the dog, he would just raise Cain with us. It didn't seem like he even cared if we, his children, had food or not. Those things have really branded themselves on my heart. When he sobered up, he would go back to work. He always seemed to have a job.

My father was a great man when he was sober. I remember late one night when he came home from drinking, and my older brother and I heard him beating up our mom. We weren't sure what to do. My brother and I talked about it, and the next morning we went into my father's bedroom. I think I was twelve at the time, my brother was fourteen. We went into the room where my dad was getting dressed. We stood cowering, in front of the large man and said, "Dad, don't you ever ever hit our mother again. If you do, you will have to fight us." Well, he never hit her again after that, and a year later they were divorced.

I don't remember my father doing more than one or two kind things for my mother and very few for the rest of the family. However, he is the only man I have ever been able to call "Dad." My father-in-law wanted me to call him "Dad," but something deep down inside of me would not let me do it. I love my father, but I'm not sure if he loved me. I cared a great deal for my dad and wanted to be friends with him, I guess, as much as with anyone in the world. I think while he was still at home we all tried to make it with dad. Still, living without love from my father was very difficult for me to handle as a young man.

I remember one particular church meeting, when I was about fourteen, a group of us youth were getting out of hand. The bishop stood in front of us and said, "I think you need to settle down. We've got a message for you and we would like you to listen to it." He went on to say, "Some of you in this room will probably be bishops and some stake presidents, and one of you may be a General Authority." The girls in the class really roared to think any of us boys had that kind of potential. I guess the one who may have laughed the hardest was my future wife. She just couldn't believe it. It's embarrassing to tell you that I came from that kind of a home. If you were to ask the bishop or someone else in the ward which of us would be the bishop or a stake president, my name, I'm sure wouldn't have even been on the list.

As a General Authority of the Church, I share these stories with you to give you a sense of hope. You may appreciate hearing them if you have lived, or currently live, under similar circumstances to my family's. Some of you may think every General Authority comes from either Joseph Fielding Smith's family or the Young's, that perhaps these slots are reserved for particular people. I think there are some people on whose shoulders the Lord gently places His hand. I guess it doesn't matter where we come from. I had an alcoholic father and came from a divorced home. While growing up, I sometimes wondered if it were possible for me to do anything in the Church. I felt inferior. Somehow, though, it doesn't matter where we come from. God will reach out his hand and place it on our shoulders.

To those of you who have been through such a terrible experience with a parent such as mine, we love you. We pray for you and we understand. We find you pure and guiltless before God. We are confident that the Lord will find you without blemish, and that His love will encircle you and bring peace to your overburdened soul. You can live without love, but you can't live without hope. What I am saying is that if the Lord will take a scroungy little kid like I was, who had to wear nurse's shoes to church, and beg for groceries, and call him to be a high counselor, a stake president, a second counselor in the Presiding Bishopric and a member of he First Quorum of the Seventy, believe that He can do just as much for you.

Develop a Job-like attitude in all you do. Job was a great soul, who said, "*though he [God] slay me, yet will I trust in him*" (Job 13:15). If we have that kind of attitude, it doesn't matter what we go through; our reward is certain in the next life. I don't believe God would put us down here and not give us any help. In closing, I call down a blessing from God to bless you with beings on the other side of the veil who will be there to help you and give you strength. My prayers will be with you.

CHAPTER FIVE

IN THE NAME OF LOVE
(A Personal Story of Codependence)

Codependency is a character trait I seem to always have had. I find myself worrying about other people, places, and things above my own needs. I find I'm unable to let other people seek out the solutions to their own problems. Also, I especially find it hard to allow others to face the consequences of their own decisions. I don't like to see other people's pain and suffering, so I step in and try to fix their problems instead of allowing them the dignity to do it themselves. I have spent my time worrying and trying to fix others over things I had no control over. Hence, this is what codependence has been to me in my life.

With codependency, I have always felt that there was something wrong with me if people I loved had problems, especially alcoholic ones. I believed I was self-sufficient enough to change others because I had all the answers. If something didn't work, I thought it was only a matter of time before I found something that would.

I grew up in a large family as one of the youngest daughters, so everyone older than me always took care of me. I basically led a sheltered life where drugs and alcohol had no place. In fact, we rarely even took aspirin or cold remedies. We were very strong in the Church, and I believed that if you just married in the temple, everything would turn out fine. I had the perfect scenario of my future planned out years before I even married.

I did get married in the temple and had several very happy years. Then my husband was critically injured in a tragic car accident and expected to never walk again. Because he was in so much pain, the doctors put him on morphine and its derivatives for a solid month. Finally, a few days before his release, a nurse told me that his bizarre behaviors in the hospital were probably a result of the drugs he had been taking. While there, some days he had been quite mean. Often he acted crazy. The nurse told me they were now stopping the drugs cold turkey, so I should expect him to be quite irritable. No one besides this nurse told me about the possibilities of addiction to these hard drugs and their side effects. And the only reason she even mentioned it was that her husband had just gone through a similar experience.

This was my first exposure to anyone who had been on hard prescription drugs. I knew he was in pain and that the painkiller they sent him home with worked. When he started going through his prescriptions quite rapidly, I was always right there to call for a new one. He had several doctors who gave him pain medication. None of them checked with the others to see if medications might interact. And because I was such a slow learner, I never even thought about this possibility. We even had some family and friends who would call in prescriptions after hours. It was all done in the name of friendship and love to help out a loved one in great pain. Addiction was not a current topic in those days, and no one really wondered why so much medication was needed. My husband always told me that because he was such a big person, he needed twice the medication to work for him. It made sense to me.

The great power of denial began to weave its dreadful web. My husband continued doing irrational things like having his body cast prematurely removed at the risk of causing great injury to himself and wandering around the neighborhood in a stupor, not even knowing his way home. Once a family member found him early one cold winter morning under his car with only a pair of Levis on. One day I even returned from work to find him on the floor with his eyes rolled back and with a large gash on his forehead. He had just gotten a new strain of painkillers that day and had overdosed. I called a close friend instead of an ambulance because I couldn't face the humiliation of an ambulance rushing into our apartment complex. In fact, I was so embarrassed I couldn't even tell my family and friends about the incident. I thought this strange behavior was just part of the drugs' side effects and believed they would just go away.

Me friend and I *did* call poison control and monitored him until all danger had passed. I look back on that incident with much horror, because I now realize how dangerous the situation was and how pride and denial kept me from doing the right things.

This episode did cause me to suspect that something was wrong, but I did nothing about it. I kept thinking that everything would just work itself out. By now, another dreadful arm of codependency was coming into play that of control. I guess I had always tried to control situations. I wanted things done my way because I felt "my way" was the only right way to do things. I liked it when everyone agreed with me and the things I said. I had mapped out my life the way I wanted it to go. Now things weren't so blissful, but I was bound and determined to change them. Little did I know that I was far from stopping an uncontrollable problem. In my innocence, I knew nothing about addiction and its crippling effect on the family members.

My husband's medical sources for prescription drugs began running low. He soon found that alcohol served the same purpose as a pain controller and depressant. It wasn't until months later that I even discovered he had started drinking. When I did, I made him promise to never do it again, and he agreed. Again, I justified the drinking as a way to stop his physical pain. Months turned into several years before I became aware that his drinking was escalating, not stopping. Menthol cough drops, mouthwashes, and eye drops can do a lot to coverup the signs. I had never really been exposed to drinking people while growing up, so I was usually fooled. And even though I sensed what was going on, I was in such a state of denial that I refused to face the truth.

I began a serious effort to control the alcoholic and his behavior. I didn't want anyone to know what kind of horrible secret we had in our home. When the drinking was more obvious, I would always wind up in a fight with the alcoholic. I made him promise to quit drinking by pleading, scolding, punishing, and threatening. I told him if we just prayed harder, the drinking would just stop. Then I would end the conversation with a threat of divorce if he didn't comply. He always promised me that there would be no more drinking and I would be satisfied. Then there would be peaceful days ahead until the situation repeated itself.

I used many things to try to control the alcoholic. I phoned excuses in frequently at work. I drove him to work. I hid car keys. I crushed antabuse into his alcohol. I constantly searched the house for any bottles so I could dump them out. I became a great detective in finding out where and what my husband was doing. If one thing didn't work, I would try something else. Several times he pleaded for help, but I always thought I could do something more to help him because I didn't want anyone to know our "secret." Besides, deep down inside, I believed I would be a failure if I couldn't stop him from drinking.

My time was consumed with the alcoholic and what he was doing. I was constantly worrying, calling, crying, or screaming and I didn't share these feelings with anyone. Several times I came close, but stopped short because of my fear that people would know I wasn't perfect, that in fact I had a great problem in my household, especially a problem that was against church standards. I became withdrawn from all my friends and family and began to take out all my frustration on my children, by yelling at them over little incidents. Then I would feel guilty for not being a "good" mom. I felt I needed to work harder in the PTA, do more in my Church jobs and do more in general so that I could be "blessed" with sobriety.

Finally, the alcoholism took a downslide. There was a DUI, a job loss, and more health problems. Our marriage held on only by a thread. The state required counseling and requested both of us attend as a part of the DUI restitution. I remember walking into the counselor's office with hate in my eyes. "Why did I need counseling? My husband was the one with the problem not me." I honestly felt that *if the drinking would just stop, all would be peaceful and happy again*, and my "blissful" scenario could then start again. The counselor looked at me and told me I was addicted to the alcoholic, and I needed help too. At that time I thought he was crazy. But I began to learn about addiction through all the films we watched during the counseling sessions, and my eyes began to open a little.

After this year of counseling had ended, I hit my own "bottom." We had just finished a few months of sobriety when the alcoholic started to act really strange. I knew he was going out to drink. One night, I pleaded with him not to go out. I just knew what was going to happen. I even grabbed onto the car door as he drove out of the driveway to try to stop the car. I stormed into the house and wrote in a notebook. The kids were already asleep, so I rehearsed my "divorce speech" and paced the floor. Of course, I tried to sleep but sleep wouldn't come. Finally at 3 a.m. I heard the car pull into the driveway. When my husband opened the door, I started my tirade. There I was, screaming and yelling at a person who was too drunk to even hear me. I threw the notebook with my "famous letter" in it. It was then that I thought I was actually mentally losing it. I stopped for a moment and saw myself as this crazy, mad woman. It was then I decided that I *did* need help.

Fortunately, my husband knew he needed help and began going to a treatment center. He had previously told the "secret" to both of our parents and to priesthood leaders. The family support group at the treatment center couldn't wait to start working on me. They couldn't believe the denial I was in and the lack of knowledge I had of my alcoholic's addiction. My eyes really started to open now. With their encouragement, I attended my first 12-step group. I wore dark glasses because I cried all through the meeting, and I didn't want anyone to recognize me. The people were wonderful, and they encouraged me to go back. I did.

The years have now passed since these episodes. I found a home in 12-step groups like Alanon and S.A.V.E. My recovery began because I learned that I played a part in the whole cycle of addiction, too. I honestly believed that after the first treatment center, we could put alcoholism into our back pockets and never face its evil again. How wrong I was. With the help of others, I realized that it had taken time to get into this mess and it would take time to dig out and rebuild our lives. We weren't part of the fortunate few who found sobriety the first time around, either. It has been a long road of treatment and relapse and recovery. However, the periods of sobriety and serenity have gotten longer each time for both the alcoholic and myself. I have since learned that I slip back into codependence just as he slips back into alcoholism, and I have to work on a program to maintain my serenity.

One of the greatest problems I have faced in my recovery is that I tend to only do well with my program when the alcoholic is also doing well with his program. I had to learn to base my own happiness on myself, and not on others. If I want a good day, I need to make it that way. It was hard to learn to detach myself from the alcoholic because I had spent so much time intertwining my life with his as I tried to control him. The realization that I was still a good person whether or not he was drinking came to me one day.

After about one year of Alanon, I actually felt like a great burden was being lifted from my shoulders. I was beginning to realize that I didn't need to take care for everyone else and their problems. I remember getting ready for a camping trip, and I let everyone help and get their own equipment. It was so nice! I didn't even plan the menus. Before, I would have spent a day making lists and getting everything ready all by myself. I was always exhausted before we had even left.

I was also learning that I didn't need to control other people and their problems. It was a new idea for me to know that I didn't have to give my advice to every friend or family member. I learned that no one grows when they are told how to solve their problems. Rather, they grow by finding their own solutions. Besides, my opinions weren't necessarily right, and they didn't need to be. I learned to shut my mouth and *listen* more to others.

Another problem I have tried to work through is letting others suffer their own consequences. I had never been able to watch others suffer, so I was always quick to rescue them from their pain. The alcoholic always knew he could count on me to get him out of sticky situations. I would make a phone call, take over a ball practice at the last moment, or run around rescuing him from any problem. I would cancel my plans if he needed help. Now, I realize that it is often only by pain that we grow or change our ways. Our Heavenly Father lets us grow through our trials, especially the ones we create ourselves.

Codependency kept me trapped in the perception that I was not okay because those around me made mistakes. I didn't allow myself to not be the perfect mother or wife. I felt a tremendous amount of shame-based guilt that I was a failure because my husband was an alcoholic. I couldn't accept myself or him as a child of God who was a human with problems. Moreover, I couldn't share my feelings with anyone outside of the program, especially those in the Church, whom I felt was constantly judging me.

I remember one of my good friends telling me about an active LDS acquaintance who had taken up drinking. She was commenting on how awful this person was. My heart sank as I vowed never to discuss my problems with her for fear she would think the same of someone I dearly loved. I also heard rumors of what Church members were saying about us. All these times I felt like staying away from church and just not facing anyone. Through lots of meetings and help from our Heavenly Father, I worked on acceptance of myself and my husband as human beings. I learned that I'm not responsible for what others choose to do, and that I make mistakes too. I learned to love those around me again because they may not understand alcoholism and its gripping effect on the alcoholic. I learned that those with the most spite often have had similar or more serious problems to face. After I began to open up and share my feelings, others did too. Many of those I had held on a pedestal began sharing their problems with me, and I learned that since we are human, it is all right to make mistakes and that we need the help of each other to overcome our obstacles.

In dealing with alcoholism, I learned to focus on myself through a 12-step program. Sometimes I would go to a meeting and think I hadn't gained anything. However, in times of hardship, the words of one of the members or a slogan from a meeting would come to my mind. This would be enough to help me through those times of extra trials.

A slogan I like for times of crisis is "Do what you normally would be doing." I remind myself of this and find that if I stay busy, my mind stays off my problems. Another one that has helped me is to "Keep mind and body in one place." In other words, concentrate on what you should be doing and force yourself to do just that. Choosing a later time to worry about my problems has really helped.

"Let go and let God" is another of my favorite sayings. I have to remember that our Heavenly Father loves the alcoholic more than I do. When I can turn the alcoholic over to our Heavenly Father's care, I leave the responsibility of the alcoholic's actions to himself. Essentially, it means that I humble myself to accept the "Lord's will,"

]not "my will." I don't try to force solutions to the problem. I don't know what the alcoholic needs to go though in this life, so I need to allow him the dignity to stumble through his own consequences. I need to remember that if I have faith in the Lord, He will show me what I need to know about the alcoholic and his behavior. He will help me know how to cope with the problem if I can clear my mind by "letting go and letting God."

Last of all, when I am in the throws of dealing with addiction, Satan would have me give up. When there is one bad day, it is so easy to think that the next day can only be as bad, if not worse. I can easily be drawn into feeling sorry for myself and in thinking I am quite a victim. Neither belief lets me think about myself and my own eternal progression, and I quickly give up working on my own program because I'm consumed in hurt and sorrow over someone else's actions. Faith and hope that tomorrow can bring sobriety need to permeate my thoughts. By allowing my Heavenly Father to care for the alcoholic, my burden can be lifted.

Chapter Six

Self-Love
The Hidden Treasure

The codependent behaviors discussed in Chapter Three are viewed as common behaviors exhibited by codependents adjusting to addiction. Some surrounding loved ones adjust to the disease of addiction by manifesting these behaviors in an attempt to demonstrate, to the best of their ability, their *love* toward the addict. These codependents are almost always trying to do what they believe is right. Simply stated, they are doing the best they can with what resources and knowledge they have available. After all they are not trained addiction specialists. The next chapters offer some information and suggestions about how to replace the codependent behaviors of rescuing, persecuting, and suffering with more effective demonstrations of love.

Everyone has asked himself at one time or another what is the greatest goal man can achieve. Of all the wonderful things life has to offer which is the supreme gift? Which one ought to be our eternal pursuit? The world might have us believe money, power, and riches would be respectable final tributes to take home to our God. Religion might suggest that going to church every Sunday, dressed in Sunday best, is our ultimate aspiration, or to be perfect in faith, service, repentance and knowledge. Well, if we believe these gifts are the greatest, we are wrong. The scriptures are very clear in identifying the greatest achievement any of us can pursue is *LOVE.*

Learning how to love the unlovable is essential if you live with an addict. Throughout the scriptures, great significance is placed on love. In 1 Nephi 11:22 the *Tree of Life* is described as "the most desirable above all things" and is defined as the "Love of God." Peter says, "Above all things have fervent charity among yourselves" (1 Peter 4:8). And remember the profound remark which Paul makes: "Love is the fulfilling of the law" (Romans 13:10). The Lord tells us in Galatians 5:14: "For all the law is fulfilled in one word, even in this; Thou shalt love thy neighbor as thyself." Additionally, in the New Testament John says, "God is Love" (1 John 4:8).

The most effective and total intervention strategy, one which never fails, is charity. The scriptures tell us that "charity never faileth" (Moroni 7:46). That is, if one wants to help someone such as an addict, who has strayed from the path the best thing he or she can do is learn to "love as God loves." Charity and loving as God loves are synonymous. The best solution to intervening with an addict comes when you use God's kind of love.

Certainly, volumes could be written on learning to love as God loves. Codependency is Satan's counterfeit form of God's love. If we are to overcome codependency, we must replace it with God's kind of love. There are many characteristics of God's love, but three seem vital in recovering from codependence. The following pages discuss these attributes, the first of which is *Self-Love*.

The final stage of codependence is represented with suffering behaviors. These are displayed by people who suffer the consequences of the addict's irresponsible actions. Remember, suffering behaviors include guilt, inadequacy, unworthiness, and shame. Frequently, such behaviors lead to the continued misuse of substances by the addict and further loss of self-esteem for loved ones. Recovery starts when the persons who play supporting roles of rescuing, persecuting and suffering begin to respond with self-love. Self-love is an initial and critical attitude for codependents to develop.

The behavior of focusing on one's self is for many members of the LDS Church very difficult to accept and even more difficult to perform. Often loved ones say such things as, "Isn't it wrong to love your self?" "Aren't self-love and selfishness the same?" "But, I feel guilty if I do things for myself." "I thought I was responsible for the addict's recovery." Self-love must replace the suffering behaviors if codependents are to begin recovery and be helpful to the addict in any fashion.

HIDDEN TREASURES

So valuable is love that the Lord has intentionally hidden some of its characteristics. Throughout time, Christ has hidden treasures from the Saints, requiring us to "seek" them if we are to have them. The concept of "hidden treasures" is suggested by a scripture found in D&C 89:19: "And shall find wisdom and great treasures of knowledge, even hidden treasures...." The most obvious example of hiding knowledge occurs in the New Testament when Christ uses parables. There are some parts to the Gospel that we can only understand if we "seek" by *keeping the commandments and feasting upon the words of Christ.* A correct understanding of self-love is one of those hidden treasures. The following can help you find this hidden gift.

THE LOVE FORMULA

Loving your neighbor as yourself is a principle taught in numerous scriptures, including Matthew 19:19, Leviticus 19:18, Matthew 22:39, Mark 12:31, Romans 13:9, Galatians 5:14, James 2:8, D&C 59:6, and D&C 112:11. Mark's version says this:

> And thou shalt love the Lord thy God with all thy heart, and with all thy soul, and with all thy mind, and with all thy strength: this is the first commandment. And the second is like, namely this, Thou shalt love thy neighbor as thyself. There is none other commandment greater than these. (Mark 12: 30-31).

As illustrated below, the Lord is teaching us in this scripture that there are *three* commandments telling us who to love.

1. Thou shalt love the Lord thy God.
2. Thou shalt love thy neighbor.

And the hidden treasure:
3. Thou shalt love thyself.

If we use an algebraic example, and allow each of the three commandments to be represented by a letter, then the "Love Formula" might be written as $A = B = C$. This formula suggests that the love we have for A should be the same love we have for B and C. The scriptures teach us that there is support for the "Love Formula." For example, in 1 John 4:20-21, we learn that in order to love God we must also love our neighbor.

A (Love for God) = B (Love for neighbor)

> If a man say, I love God, and hateth his brother, he is a liar: for he that loveth not his brother whom he hath seen, how can he love God whom he hath not seen? And this commandment have we from him, That he who loveth God love his brother also.

Golden Rule.
In addition, the Golden Rule says, "Do unto others as you would have them do unto you." Love thy neighbor as thyself.

B (Love for neighbor) = C (Love for self)

One might ask, "How do I really live the Golden Rule?" Do you really "love yourself" as well or as effectively as you love your neighbor or your God, as is suggested in the Love Formula? Often, Mormons forget this great principle and believe they can love God or their neighbor without "loving themselves." In your most inner thoughts are you making many negative self comments? Many members of the LDS Church equate humility with self-degradation. For example, if someone says, "You gave a good talk," you reply: "Oh no I didn't. It was nothing." Some believe the way to obtain humility is by continually running one's self down. It is a blessing that some of us don't treat our neighbor as we do ourselves because our homes and our neighborhoods would be much worse. Our families and communities would be flooded with negative and rude statements.

A Model of Self-Love

One extreme of self-love can best be characterized with an understanding of narcissism. Narcissism is a selfish wicked form of love for "self." Greek mythology can help us to understand this concept.

Selfish example.
Narcissus was a handsome young man who despised love. The best known version is that of Ovid's *Metamorphoses*. Narcissus was the object of the passions of many girls and Nymphs, but he was indifferent to it all. The Nymph, Echo, fell in love with him but she could get no more from him than the others could. In despair, she withdrew into a lonely spot where she faded away until all that was left of her was her sorrowful voice. The girls rejected by Narcissus asked the heavens for vengeance. Nemesis heard them and arranged so that one very hot day Narcissus bent over a stream to take a drink and saw his own face, which was so handsome he immediately fell in love with it. From then on he stayed there watching his own reflection until he died. Narcissism occurs when a person becomes so preoccupied about working out his or her own serenity, that the salvation of others and the personal relationship with God is neglected and jeopardized.

Bruce R. McConkie, in *Mormon Doctrine*, sees selfishness as,

> consisting in caring unduly or supremely to oneself; it is one of the lusts of the flesh which must be overcome. A selfish person clings to his own comfort, advantage, or position at the expense of others.

We are commanded to repent from such pride, selfishness, and narcissism.

Selfless example.
Codependence is the other extreme of self-love. It is a wicked form of loving others. It occurs when one becomes so preoccupied about working out another's salvation that one's own salvation becomes neglected or jeopardized. A personal experience can teach this concept. As a psychologist, I often have the opportunity to be in psychiatric

wards. I recall one occasion on which a good member of the Church was hospitalized. The referring psychiatrist described her as having so over-extended herself in serving others that she had experienced what many would call a nervous breakdown. I arrived at the hospital early Saturday morning and began to look for this patient. She wasn't in her room or on the wing. As I poked my head into her assigned room all I saw was a small pile of what appeared to be dirty laundry on her bed. I inquired at the nurse's desk and discovered that this good sister was across the hall doing the laundry of fellow patients. This Relief Society sister always went the "extra mile" regardless of her personal circumstances. If the bishop needed her to visit someone or do something, she was always there. She would leave her home immediately when called upon, whether eating dinner with her family, reading her scriptures, or even while praying. Even while in the hospital, she was found doing the laundry of the other patients, while her own laundry was left undone. This sister truly lost herself in the service of others. Perhaps the Self-Love Meter on the next page can assist you in distinguishing between the two extremes of self-love.

SELF-LOVE METER

SELFISH   **100**
(NARCISSISM)
- No Pleasure in Giving
- Interest Only in Self
- Wants Everything for Self
- Sees Nothing But Self
- Overlooks Needs of Others
- Avoids Personal Pain
- Withdrawn Love From Others and Turned it Toward Self
- Is Distant From God

SELF-ESTEEM   **50**
- Receives/Gives with Pleasure
- Interested in Self & Others
- Is Close to God
- Seeks Spiritual Growth

SELFLESS   **0**
(CODEPENDENCE)
- No Pleasure in Receiving
- Interest Only in Others
- Wants Everything for Others
- Sees Nothing But Others
- Overlooks Needs of Self
- Helps Others Avoid Pain
- Withdrawn Love From Self and Turned it Toward Others
- Is Distant From God

Somewhere between narcissism and codependence is a healthy kind of self-love. Elder Dean L. Larsen states,

> We are like all others in some respects, each of us is unique. There has never been anyone exactly like you. There never will be. Never will anyone possess your special individuality and your particular possibilities....*It is necessary to accept ourselves with a self-love that is neither vain nor selfish*, but rather one that is tolerant and understanding, one that we might feel toward an old friend....Part of enduring to the end is related to our attitudes toward ourselves. When we have a high enough regard for ourselves, we can overcome setbacks and still go forward. ("The Peaceable Things of the Kingdom", Feb. 1986, *The New Era*, p. 3, *emphasis added*. © Copyright by The Church of Jesus Christ of Latter-day Saints. Used by permission.)

A healthy self-love is neither selfish or selfless. There is a widespread belief that, while it is virtuous to love others, it is sinful to love oneself. It is assumed by many that the degree to which people love themselves directly reflects how much they do *not* love others. That in all cases self-love is the same as selfishness and we, as members of the Church, must avoid all types of self-love. This is not the case. It is interesting to note that the Book of Mormon uses the word "esteem" instead of "love." The concept of esteem is taught clearly in Mosiah 27:4: "That every man should esteem his neighbor as himself..." For some of us it is perhaps easier to work toward "esteeming"-ourselves than "loving"-ourselves." Regardless of the term used, "esteem" or "love," the process of respecting self is essential to begin the process of recovery.

The love for one's self is inseparably connected with the love for any other being, including God, as is suggested by the Love Formula. The attribute of love taught by this formula is, "One's love for others and God rarely rises above one's love for self." This hidden treasure suggests that it is as important a commandment to "love thy self" as it is to "love thy God" and "love thy neighbor." In fact, one cannot love one's neighbor, spouse, children, or God more than one loves oneself (1 John 4:20-21). Romans 14:22, encourages us by saying: "Hast thou faith? Have it to thyself before God...."

EMOTIONAL AND SPIRITUAL SELF-RELIANCE

In 1990 the LDS Church published a welfare manual entitled *Providing in the Lord's Way*. This document "...explains the way the Lord has revealed for his saints to care for themselves..." and suggests that "...we cannot give what we do not have" (p. 1). President Kimball goes on to explain the principle of self-reliance:

> The responsibility for each person's social, emotional, spiritual, physical, or economic well-being rests first upon himself....No true Latter-day Saint, while physically or emotionally able will voluntarily shift the burden of his own or his family's well-being to someone else. So long as he can, under the inspiration of the Lord and with his own labors, he will supply himself and his family with the spiritual and temporal necessities of life. (Conference Report, Oct. 1977, p. 124; or *Ensign*, Nov. 1977, pp 77-78. © Copyright by The Church of Jesus Christ of Latter-day Saints. Used by permission.)

The importance of self-reliance is a cornerstone of understanding both our religion and codependence.

> There is much talk of governmental or other organized provisions for our wants, material and spiritual, when in reality our greatest needs must be satisfied with ourselves. To lean upon others for support enfeebles the soul. By self-effort man will attain his highest destiny. It cannot be placed as a cape upon his shoulders by others. Upon his own feet he must enter into the Kingdom of God whether on heaven or earth. By conquest of self he must win his own place in the everlasting glory of God's presence. (Elder Melvin J. Ballard, *Sermons and Missionary Services of M.J. Ballard*. 1949, p. 136. © Copyright by The Church of Jesus Christ of Latter-day Saints. Used by permission.)

Notice in the first quote that President Kimball speaks of emotional and spiritual welfare on an equal level with temporal welfare. In addition, Elder Ballard clearly lists spiritual needs in conjunction with material ones. As members of the Church we can easily understand the importance of being temporally self-reliant. But can we equally understand the importance of emotional and spiritual self-reliance? The concept of temporal self-reliance is simple. The more financially reliant we are on others, the less freedom we have to spend our money on what we want. If I have $20 given to me as a gift and have $400 worth of bills how much freedom do I have to spend the $20? If I have no food storage and a large earthquake occurs how much freedom do I have to eat? Welfare principles apply to both spiritual and emotional preparedness.

Jethro teaching Moses.

If I have invested all my esteem, my love, my time and my effort in working out or worrying about someone else's salvation, how much time and energy do I have left to work out my own? In Exodus 17, the Lord teaches this principle to Moses. The story begins with Jethro, Moses' father-in-law, bringing Moses' wife and sons to meet him. While visiting Jethro, Moses' father-in-law becomes aware of Moses' codependency.

> And it came to pass on the morrow, that Moses sat to judge the people: and the people stood by Moses from the morning unto the evening. And when Moses' father in law saw all that he did to the people he said, What is this thing that thou doest to the people? why sittest thou thyself alone, and all the people stand by thee from morning unto even? And Moses said unto his father in law, Because the people come unto me to enquire of God; When they have a matter they come unto me; and I judge between one and another, and I do make them know the statues of God, and his laws. (Exodus 18: 13-16)

One might wonder "What is Jethro worried about? Isn't Moses doing the Lord's work from sun up to sun down? What more can one do? Surely God would approve of such behavior?" Jethro, being inspired of the, Lord counsels Moses:

> And Moses' father in law said unto him, *the thing that thou does is not good.* Thou wilt surely wear away, both thou, and this people that is with thee: for this thing is too heavy for thee; thou are not able to perform it thyself alone. (Exodus 18: 17-18, *emphasis added.*)

Jethro recognized that Moses would eventually "wear away" if he continued doing everything himself. Perhaps he might of ended up having a nervous breakdown like the Relief Society sister discussed above. Jethro instructed Moses to appoint lesser judges and to delegate power to them. Then Jethro gave Moses a promise:

> If thou shalt do this thing, and God command thee so, then thou shalt be able to endure, and all this people shall also go to their place in peace. (Exodus 18:23)

An important component of self-love is taking time to be emotionally self-reliant. Ask yourself, "What would happen to my emotional stability if my spouse sought a divorce?" "Will I be emotionally self-reliant and survive this hardship?" "Will I have a nervous breakdown?" "What if a loved one abuses alcohol or drugs? Do I have enough spiritual and emotional self-reliance to continue working out my own salvation?" These are questions we should ask ourselves to determine the extent of our emotional and spiritual preparedness.

Personal salvation.
As the Apostle Paul counseled us in Phillipians 2:12, "Work out your own salvation with fear and trembling before God." I know of no place in LDS doctrine where a son or daughter of God is asked to sacrifice his or her personal salvation for another. We may be asked to sacrifice our time, property, money, and even our lives, but not our personal salvation. Remember, *codependency occurs when a person becomes so focused upon or preoccupied with working out another person's salvation that his or her own salvation becomes neglected and jeopardized.* Abraham labored that his own father would overcome transgression. Despite his best efforts, his father turned to idolatry. Had Abraham let that proper concern for a father consume his every thought, he could not have received this promise: "In thy seed shall all the kindreds of the earth be blessed " (3 Nephi 20:25). Where might we be now if Abraham had been codependent and did not obtain his personal exaltation because he was too busy working out his father's exaltation?

In Galatians 6:4-5 we read, "But let every man prove his own work, and then shall he have rejoicing in himself alone, and not in another. For every man shall bear his own burden." President Romney reiterates this simple concept:

> Let us be self-reliant and independent. Salvation can be obtained on no other principle. Salvation is an individual matter, and we must work out our own salvation, in temporal as well as in spiritual things. (Marion G. Romney, *Ensign*, November 1976, p. 124. © Copyright by The Church of Jesus Christ of Latter-day Saints. Used by permission.)

Juel G., a codependent, states: "You are responsible for your ability to love but not for the outcome of another's life." He goes on to say that the outcome of the addict's life must be dependent on his or her choices and responses. A parent or spouse who prays, goes to church, pays tithing, has family home evening and obeys all the other commandments has only one guarantee: That they have become a perfect parent or spouse, not that they will necessarily have perfect children or a perfect marriage partner. Another way to view this concept in relationship to a marriage partner is to remember: *It is your primary responsibility to be a celestial mate, not to make your mate celestial.*

HOW DOES ONE DEVELOP SELF-LOVE?

1. SPEND TIME ALONE

One must take time to be alone in order to develop self-love. In Matthew 7:3 Jesus said: "And why beholdest thou the mote that is in thy brother's eye, but considerest not the beam that is in thine own eye?" Codependents must focus on the "beam" in their own lives before various strategies and interventions aimed toward the "mote" in the addict's life will be effective. Each of us needs to understand that our first priority is to return ourselves to our Heavenly Father and make the necessary changes in our life to do just that. In part, this is done by taking time to be alone. Each codependent must become sufficiently self-reliant to work out his or her personal salvation in a private fashion, as Joseph Smith did in the Sacred Grove, as Moses did on Mount Sinai, as Enos did in the forest, and as Christ did in the wilderness. If our personal "spirituality bucket," is empty what can we offer those around us who are in need of "living water?"

Certainly, it is difficult to make time for ourselves in such a busy world. The needs of the Church, our children, and our spouses, can be demanding. In order to be alone, at times important tasks will have to be postponed or even left undone. Consider what happened to the Israelites while Moses went alone to Mount Sinai. They began worshipping idols. Someone surely would have benefitted from a blessing while Christ was in the desert alone for 40 days and nights? Did someone have to do Joseph Smith's chores while he was in the Grove? However inconvenient, these absences (when men took time to be alone and with God) benefitted the entire human race in the ways that can't be measured.

Perhaps the best scriptural example illustrating the importance of being alone is found in Matthew 14:22-23. Here disciples tell Jesus that John the Baptist has been beheaded "...When Jesus heard of it, he departed thence by ship into a desert place apart..." But the people heard where Jesus was going and they followed him by the thousands. Jesus ministered unto the 5,000 "beside women and children" and fed them. After the miracle of feeding the onlookers, the scriptures tell us:

> And straightway Jesus constrained his disciples to get into a ship, and to go before him unto the other side, while he sent the multitudes away. And when he had sent the multitudes away, he went up into a mountain apart to pray; and when the evening was come, he was there alone. (*emphasis added*)

The meaning is not clear but it almost seems as if Jesus had not finished sorting out His questions and feelings about John the Baptist's death. So He arranged things so that He could be alone. At times each of us "must send the multitudes away" to pray and sort through things alone.

Spending time alone with yourself and occasionally doing things for yourself are essential in developing self-love. Begin to spend a few minutes a day by yourself away from the TV, the radio, and others. Take this time to think and feel. Perhaps taking a walk around the block or simply locking yourself in your bedroom will do. This time could be spent praying or fasting, or you could do something purely fun, just for you. If possible make one of the things you do something physical. This does not mean housework. Codependents can easily find ways to continue their roles as caretakers. Don't add any more "shoulds" to your life.

For many codependents the guilt associated with spending time alone and caring for themselves will make this assignment nearly impossible to complete. However, continue your efforts in hope. If time alone is spent effectively, someday you will be able to find the "hidden treasure" YOU! You will become acquainted with your inner feelings, your aspirations the blessings promised you in your patriarchal blessing. God wants it this way. Only Satan would have you believe it is a sin to work out your own personal salvation and return to Heavenly Father.

2. SET PRIORITIES

As one spends time alone, feelings and thoughts naturally occur. A number of activities and duties may leap into your mind. The second suggestion in developing self-love is prioritizing these many obligations. Learning to set priorities is essential for the codependent. No member of the Church can fulfill 100 percent of each commandment simultaneously. One cannot be actively involved with missionary work for the living and the dead at the same time. If I'm at the temple doing an endowment, I can't be at the genealogy building doing my five-generation sheets, or at my neighbors' doing home teaching, or at home helping my daughter with her algebra. A priority list must be made, and some important "required" things *will be left undone*. You may gain some insight by reading the following quote from Brigham Young.

> Were I to draw a distinction in all the duties that are required of the children of men, from first to last, I would place first and foremost the duty of seeking unto the Lord our God until we open the paths of communications from Heaven to Earth from God to our own. (Melchizedek Priesthood Manual 1991, p. 65. © Copyright by The Church of Jesus Christ of Latter-day Saints. Used by permission.)

Many times we may be forced to choose from our "required" duties where to spend our time and energy. As mentioned none of us have the time or energy in a day to do all that is required of us. President Young very clearly states that maintaining personal communication with our Heavenly Father outweighs other items identified on the Mormon "to do list." Flight attendants instruct us that in the event of an emergency, we should put on our "own oxygen masks first" before assisting others with theirs. In the same way, our Heavenly Father expects us to have a flow of our own "spiritual air" before we attempt to assist others. (Elder Thomas Fyans, AMCAP Conference, Oct. 5, 1984).

> And if it so be that you shall labor all your days in crying repentance unto this people, and bring, save it be one soul unto me, how great shall be your joy with him in the kingdom of my Father! (D&C 18:15)

Many believe that the "one soul" referred to in this scripture is the neighbor or the nonmember whom we fellowship into the Church. It seems that our loving God would be very disappointed if we selected someone else to be the "one soul" saved. If you are forced to save only one person, that person should surely be yourself! God wants it that way. *Remember, the error of codependence isn't that you are performing Christ-like behaviors and taking care of "others". The error is you do it at the risk of neglecting yourself.*

3. FIND A FRIEND

Attempt to identify and become involved with support resources early in the process of recovery from codependence. A codependent *cannot* overcome the grasp of codependency without a support system. The powers of addiction are just too strong to escape them without help. Effective support resources should remind codependents of their divinity, eternal perspective, and self-worth, as the going gets tough in recovery. Codependents may be able to apply some of what they learn on their own. However, the typical addict presents himself with too much deception and manipulation. Initially, the codependent has too little objectivity and esteem to deal with the addict alone. So find a friend. Obvious friends include our Heavenly Father and the scriptures. Less obvious but helpful supports might come from a trusted friend, appropriate priesthood leader or sister, support groups such as Alanon or S.A.V.E., and literature relating to the topic of codependence. A periodic report to that support resource will be essential in developing and maintaining spirituality and faith in yourself throughout the recovery process.

Generally individuals should have as many support resources as possible. There should be no shortage in support groups to attend, good literature-including the scriptures-to read, and close friends to call upon.

4. SEE YOURSELF AS GOD SEES YOU

One final suggestion for developing self-love is to see yourself as God sees you. The Love Formula (A = B = C) suggests this process. Simply love yourself the same way God loves you. John 13:34 reads, "That ye love one another; as I have loved you." Might we add this: "That ye love *yourself*; as He has loved you."

We ought to see ourselves similarly to how God sees himself: with respect, esteem, and love. When God describes himself, he exhibits a healthy self-esteem. In Moses 1:3, he says,

> And God spake unto Moses saying, Behold, I am the Lord God Almighty, and endless is my name for I am without beginning of days or end of years.

Perhaps a personal equivalent of this message could be borrowed from the LDS Young Women's Value and Definition. It might read, "Behold I am a child of God... I am of infinite worth with my own divine mission which I will strive to fulfill."

Make every effort to see yourself as God might see you. Treat yourself the way God or Christ, your older brother, would treat you if they were to visit you today. Many members of the Church feel that to take time for themselves or to feel good about themselves is sinful.

God gave you life, gave you His Only Begotten Son, arranged for life on this planet, and gave you a body and talents, for which he will someday return and to ask an accounting. Those talents include your ability to maintain your sanity and serenity. You, personally, will be the one asked to give an accounting for these things. Accept the challenge of loving yourself as God loves you. There is a spark of divinity in each of us. Satan rejoices when he and his armies are able to influence us to darken our *own* divine spark by our questioning, condemning, and overly criticizing our worth and potential as God's children. As stated in Romans 14:22, "...Happy is he who condemeth not himself..."

God's love.

God's love for you and your worth as a daughter or son of God will *never* be questioned at least not by Him. Paul clearly identifies in Romans 8: 35, 38-39 the extent of Christ's love for you.

> Who shall separate us from the love of Christ? Shall tribulation, or distress, or persecution, or famine, or nakedness, or peril, or sword? For I am persuaded, that neither death, nor life, nor angels, nor principalities, nor powers, nor things present, nor things to come, nor height, nor depth, nor any other creature, shall be able to separate us from the love of God, which is in Christ Jesus our Lord.

Clearly Christ's love for the codependent shall not be hampered by the behavior of an addict. However, it can be hampered by the codependent's suffering behaviors of low self-esteem and low self-love. That is, at times the love of others, including the love of Christ, cannot be experienced by a codependent, even though Christ extends it. This occurs because the codependent is in the depths of suffering and refuses to open his heart to anyone's love. The codependent simply believes he or she is unworthy of love. Replacing suffering behaviors with self-love is an essential first step in recovery.

ROADBLOCKS

Those who can't.

In some cases, developing self-love may be difficult, if not impossible, because of personal problems. Personal problems might include not having resolved early childhood issues of your own (i.e. Adult Children of Alcoholic), a troubled marriage, or other psychosocial disorders. If such seems to be the case, a consultation with a local professional counselor might prove very helpful. Finally, there are some who will never be able to obtain this self-love through no fault of their own and regardless of their personal efforts. Some types of mental illness are so encompassing and deceiving that self-love in this life may never be achieved.

Satan's counterfeit.

Surely Satan will pervert and create opposition in all things including self-love. Narcissism and codependence are Satan's distortions of God's self-love. While prophesying about the apostasy in the last days, Paul described about twenty behaviors that man will exhibit before the Second Coming. The first is that man will become "lovers of their own selves. "...For in the last days perilous times shall come. For men shall be *lovers of their own selves...*" (2 Timothy 3:1-2, *emphasis added*). Why did Paul first list this sin. Many prophets, including President Kimball, have frequently admonished us against pride. Why are selfishness and pride such horrible sins? Developing God's kind of self-love requires us to discern the difference between Satan's version and God's version. Certainly, understanding self-love in a personal way requires a searching, fearless, effort to find the "Hidden Treasure" of God's kind of love. Each of us must be very careful to develop the healthy kind of self-love as suggested by the Self-Love Meter rather than Satan's counterfeit, narcissism.

SUMMARY

Love Attribute #1:
One's love for others and God rarely rises above one's love for self.

Scripture:
And thou shalt love the Lord thy God with all thy heart, and with all thy soul, and with all thy mind, and with all thy strength: this is the first commandment. And the second is like, namely this, Thou shalt love thy neighbor as thyself. There is none other commandment greater than these. (Mark 12: 30-31)

THE MAN IN THE GLASS

When you get what you want in your struggle for self
   And the world makes you king for the day
Just go to the mirror and look at yourself
   And see what that man has to say.
For it isn't your parents or children or wife
   Whose judgement upon you must pass
The fellow whose verdict counts most in your life
   Is the one staring back in the glass.
Some people may think you a straight-shooting chum
   And call you a wonderful guy
But the man in the glass says your only a bum
   If you can't look him straight in the eye.
He's the fellow to please, never mind the rest
   For he's with you clear up to the end.
And you've passed your most dangerous, difficult test
   If the man in the glass is your friend.
You may fool the whole world down the pathway of life
   And get pats on your back as you pass
But your final reward is heartaches and tears
   If you've cheated the man in the glass.

CHAPTER SEVEN

UNCONDITIONAL LOVE
HOLD ON WITH AN OPEN HAND

Unconditional Love is the second attribute of God's kind of love. As discussed in Chapter Three, surrounding loved ones often find themselves performing persecuting behaviors out of anger, desperation and frustration. These behaviors become the source of persecution for the addict. Such behaviors include nagging, threatening and blaming. The result of such behavior includes a further loss of self-worth and continued substance use for the addict and further loss of control and continued frustration for the loved ones.

Many codependents are waiting for the addict to take the first step and "earn" that unconditional love. But the addict will not likely take the first step because he or she by definition, is sick and has no free agency to change behavior anyway. If you are a parent, spouse, or child who has been waiting for the addict to give some expression of respect and love first, please heed this: One of the most effective secrets for helping the addict and yourself to get well is contained in the fourth chapter of 1 John 19. Only eight words long it reads: "We love Him, because He first loved us." This simple scripture suggests that we must first love the addict before he or she can love us. The following is a discussion on developing a love for the unlovable.

THE GOOD SAMARITAN

The thieves "...wounded him, and departed, leaving him half dead." The good Samaritan offered help "unto him that fell among the thieves" and took care of him, performing what was reasonable to preserve life. Then the Samaritan took the injured man to the inn and made necessary arrangements for his care and planned to check on his condition upon his return.

The story of the good Samaritan teaches us that there is a time and place to care for and love our "enemies." Through the course of the disease, the addict develops the ability to curse, hate, despitefully use and persecute the codependent. But how would the Lord have us feel toward someone who treats his children in such a way? In Matthew 5:44, Jesus teaches us,

> Love your enemies, bless them that curse you, do good to them that hate you and pray for them which despitefully use you, and persecute you.

Anyone who has lived with an addict realizes at one time or another they are the recipient of all of the above behaviors.

This ability to love unconditionally is a critical attribute of loving as God loves. Bernie Siegel, M.D., in his book *Love Medicine & Miracles* says: "Unconditional love is the most powerful stimulant of the immune system. The truth is: love heals." The LDS priesthood manual states, "No power is as motivating as the power of love" (Priesthood Manual 1990 p. 120). In addition, to self-love, unconditional love acts as another important ingredient to recovery from codependence.

PERSONALITIES BEFORE PRINCIPLES

CONDITIONAL LOVE

One of the twelve traditions of S.A.V.E. and similar twelve-step groups, involves the saying, "Principles before Personalities." This adage teaches the difference between conditional and unconditional love. In the case of codependence, the "personality" becomes more important than the "principles." Codependents tend to show respect, love, and hope if the addict is exhibiting a pleasant and acceptable "personality." But when the addict waivers by doing things the codependent despises this love and respect waivers. A codependent's love is based on the addict's behavior, not on the correct principle of unconditional love.

AN EXAMPLE

Following is a story of a father who placed his son's addicted personality before the principle of unconditional love. This codependent father found there was a limit to his love.

A high priest and his family were sitting in church during Fast and Testimony meeting. Not seated with them was one of their older boys who was about 19 and well into the last stages of addiction. When unexpectedly, this son walked into the chapel and took a seat at the back of the chapel, the father felt his prayers had been answered. He felt hope and acceptance toward his son. Then, during the course of the meeting, the son began to walk toward the front of the chapel to share his testimony as those before him had done. It was only then that the father recognized the familiar stagger of his son's intoxication. The love and gratitude he had felt only minutes before now quickly faded into anger and hate.

His son was drunk, and he was headed for the pulpit. With each step, the father's anger and embarrassment grew. The boy stepped behind the pulpit and began sharing his testimony. By now the father could hardly contain himself and fervently prayed that "God might take this moment away." The son was so obviously drunk that everyone in the ward knew. During the middle of the boy's testimony, he passed out and fell at the feet of the bishopric. The father's heart fell, too. This was the last straw, the behavior that made the dad stop loving his son. The pain, embarrassment, and guilt was so extreme the father made a promise that he would never be hurt again by his son's drinking. He bought some eyebolts and chains the next day, intending to chain his son to the basement wall until he sobered up.

This story shows how the father's first love and acceptance for his son changed to anger and hatred in a matter of minutes. The father was a helpless victim of the addict's personality *and* his personal codependence. There was no room for correct principles. One might ask, "Who was more sick?" or "Who had the greater sin?" "Was it the father, who had intentions to chain his son to the wall, or was it the son, who passed out while sharing his testimony?"

Unconditional love asks the question: "What kind of loved one are you that you only love addicts when they do what you want them to do?" It is a selfish, self-centered, conditional, and qualified love! It is easy to love the addict when he or she is clean, sober, and repentant. But when he or she relapses, our love is needed even more. Unconditional love suggests that we should love no matter the behavior. In Matthew 5:45, we read: "For if ye love them which love you, what reward have ye?"

PRINCIPLES BEFORE PERSONALITIES

A codependent in recovery will work at accepting the higher principle of unconditional love and say, "I love you more than I hate the things that you do." Or, in other words, "I place the principle of unconditional love before your addictive personality." Recovering codependents will remind themselves in relationship to the addict that, "You cannot sin enough, drink enough, scream enough, lie enough, steal enough to make me stop loving you!" Is there a limit to your love? How much sin does it take for you to stop loving your spouse, parent, or child? (It is important to note that this does *not* mean the codependent is required to accept or approve, live with, or support the addict's behavior. All it means is that we must love them as sons and daughters of God.)

Elder H. Burke Peterson talks about the importance of demonstrating unconditional love in dealing with problem children. These suggestions can be equally helpful in dealing with addicts. Elder Peterson says:

> We must make an even clearer effort to communicate real love to a questioning child. The giving of love from a parent to a son or daughter must not be dependent on the child's performance. Oft times those we

think deserve our love the least need it the most. ...May I suggest that parents' teachings will be listened to more intently and be heeded more closely if they are preceded by and woven together with that golden fiber of love. If our words are to be remembered, they must be accompanied and followed by considerate, thoughtful actions that cannot be forgotten. (*Love*, Deseret Book, p. 62. © Copyright by The Church of Jesus Christ of Latter-day Saints. Used by permission.)

There are numerous examples of individuals placing the gospel principle of unconditional love before personalities. These people exhibit a love which has no limits.

Elder Rex D. Pinegar.

Elder Rex D. Pinegar offers an example of how his family demonstrated unconditional love to his father an alcohol abuser.

> Later in life, while I was a counselor in a reading clinic in Los Angeles, I learned a great lesson. They sent me older boys with reading problems. Richard was a nonreader. I asked him, "Why are we together?"
>
> "I don't know," he answered.
>
> "I really want to get to know you," I said. "I'd rather know about you than your reading. Let's assume you could be anyone you wanted to be. Who would that be?"
>
> "I want to be like my dad," Richard said without hesitation.
>
> "Why?"
>
> "Because my mother loves him," he answered.
>
> Richard's father had been in prison for 11 years. It was then I realized that this was a reiteration of what I had felt about my own father *while he was drinking.* I wanted to be like my father because my mother taught me that "someday you'll know him like I know him." My mother loved him. (*Honor Your Father*, S.A.V.E., 1984, *emphasis added*)

How is it that Elder Pinegar, who as a young man would find a bottle of Seagram 7 in his father's top dresser drawer, whose father would disappear on drinking binges for two or three days at a time, would still love him enough to want to be like him, an alcohol abuser? How could Elder Pinegar overcome his father's drinking personality? I believe that the family members' faith and love played an important role. Elder Pinegar and his family were able to follow the higher principle of love and see much deeper than the superficial drinking habits. The Pinegar family was able to "know their father as God knows him." Elder Pinegar's father eventually stopped drinking.

Christ on the Cross.
Perhaps the greatest example of unconditional love is demonstrated by Christ. Judas had betrayed him, Peter had denied him, then "soldiers stripped him and put on him a scarlet robe," then mocked and scoffed at him (Matthew 27:28,41). But as he hung on the cross, he forgave all:

> And when they were come to the place, which is called Calvary, there they crucified him...Then said Jesus, Father, forgive them; for they know not what they do. And they parted his raiment, and cast lots. (Luke 23: 33-34)

The perfect example of Christ-like love comes from Christ himself.

HOW DOES ONE DEVELOP UNCONDITIONAL LOVE?

1. FORGIVE

Forgive the addict.
Many codependents who understand the gospel realize the importance of forgiveness as part of the recovery process. Most LDS codependents know that Heavenly Father would like them to forgive the addict. Nevertheless, the pain which the addict has caused in their lives may still be intense. These codependents are unable to forgive and continue to have the void in their life caused by hate, revenge, and fear. They begin to treat their once-loved addict as an enemy. It is easy to understand why these loved ones respond with resentment, bitterness, and a withdrawing of love. After all, didn't the addict offend, mistreat, sin against, lie to, falsely accuse, neglect, and reject them? However, the Lord very clearly suggests in D&C 64:9 that the codependent who is unwilling to forgive the addict commits a greater sin than the addict.

> Wherefore, I say unto you, that ye ought to forgive one another; for he that forgiveth not his brother his trespasses standeth condemned before the Lord; for there remaineth in him the greater sin. (D&C 64:9)

Forgiveness has little to do with what the addict did or said. Forgiveness is not about the addict. It is about the codependent. Forgiveness is the ultimate act of unconditional love. Elder Marion D. Hanks describes forgiveness as the ultimate form of love for God and men. In a talk entitled "Forgiveness: The Ultimate Form of Love," Elder Hanks goes on to say:

> Even if it appears that another may be deserving of our resentment or hatred, none of us can afford to pay the price of resenting or hating because of what it does to us. If we have felt the gnawing, mordant inroads of these emotions we know the harm we suffer. So Paul taught the Corinthians that they must "see that none render evil for evil unto any man." (*LOVE*, Deseret Book, 1986 p. 93. © Copyright by The Church of Jesus Christ of Latter-day Saints. Used by permission.)

Understanding the disease of addiction is also part of forgiveness. As discussed in Chapter One, the addict has usually died a "spiritual death" and is, in the later stages of addiction, suffering from a *disease*. Codependents can find some peace and increased ability to detach when they learn about and accept in their hearts this great truth.

By forgiving the addict, the codependent can let go of some of the negative and awkward feelings that come with continual internal pain and confusion. Through forgiveness comes a sense of peace, inner harmony, and wholeness. As Claudia Black, an adult child of an alcoholic, has stated: "Forgiveness is self love, it is an act of taking care of yourself." It is important to note that even if one implements a tough love behavior of getting a divorce or calling the police, the codependent is still required to forgive the addict!

Forgive yourself.

Part of forgiving is learning how to let go and forgive yourself. The will to hate, to resent, to anger, to remorse, to feel guilt over your own performance is so powerful that it will bind you to the addict like glue. This connection of self-guilt will engulf your whole life through the eternities whether or not the addict that hurt you is around. The ability to let go of unreasonable guilt and shame dissolves the glue and allows you freedom to move on.

Feeling less guilty for your role in the addict's life helps the codependent develop unconditional love. A question often asked is, "How responsible should I be and feel for the addict's misbehaviors?" Pertinent to this question is a very important concept discussed by Brother Arthur Bassett in an article entitled "How Responsible Are Parents?" Where he discusses responsibilities of parents and spouses for the behaviors of rebellious children or partners.

> ...If you have done your best, all you have known to do, to bring that child up in the ways of the Lord even then some families will not succeed, *but through no fault of their own*. This is because of the God-given right of their children [spouses] to exercise their agency. People are not clay to be molded according to the parent's [or spouse's] will into pre-determined forms; they are not puppets who are to dance at the parent's [or spouse's] direction. They are thinking, feeling individuals, co-eternal with their parents [spouses] and capable of choosing to accept or reject the life-styles of the families in which they are... (I Have a Question. *Ensign*, June 1982, pp. 34-35. *emphasis added.* © Copyright by The Church of Jesus Christ of Latter-day Saints. Used by permission.)

Forgive vs. Forget.

Forgiving the addict and yourself does not mean that the codependent will forget. In most cases there are many horrible memories of what the addict has done to you and what you have done to the addict in the privacy of your home. The chances of these memories disappearing over time is not likely. Simply said, amnesia is not part of recovery. For example, adult children of alcoholics who had the abuse occur thirty years earlier even after working through the pain and *forgiving* still have the memories. Do not measure the healing process by how much you forget, but rather how much you are able to forgive. The healing codependent will remember the events but having forgiven the addict and themselves, will have *less* emotional pain than if they had not forgiven.

2. PERFORM SAFE-LOVE BEHAVIORS

Unconditional love is a pure attribute of Christ-like love. Above all the challenges and problems associated with living with a substance abuser, developing a pure love for them is generally the most difficult challenge of recovery. Such a love for the addict cannot be developed without divine intervention. That is, pure unconditional love, which includes the ability to forgive, can only be obtained as a gift from the Spirit. True unconditional love cannot be faked, learned from a book, or obtained from a friend. It can only be given as a gift from our Heavenly Father. The anger, hate, and resentment that typically develop within the hearts of loved ones as the addict progresses through addiction are so strong that codependents often become powerless to their great force. Only a power greater than ourselves can lift that immense burden. Unconditional love, therefore, must be obtained like any other spiritual gift through meekness, prayer, and faith. Each codependent is encouraged to seek after this "gift" if recovery is to proceed.

Such scriptures as Moroni 8:6 and Moroni 7:48 are helpful in understanding this love. The pursuit of unconditional love in some respects may take years. As a codependent, you may have to live or be around the one you "hate" (the addict) each day. You may feel there is not enough time to obtain the gift of unconditional love. The urgency to do something prompts the development of safe-love behaviors. Safe-Love behaviors occur when loved ones demonstrate their love to the addict in a clear, unmistakable way.

The "safe" part of safe love is very important to understand. Loved ones often carry anger, bitterness, hatred, and other negative emotions toward the addict to the extent that they are unable to treat the addict with respect, let alone love. It is not unusual for codependents to have to "talk themselves into" performing safe-love behaviors because the addict can be so difficult. Also, one might believe that surely the addict hasn't earned the right to be treated with respect. Therefore, the demonstration of safe love may be the best the codependent can do at this point.

Safe love is more successful when it is "safe" from the codependent's negative emotions and "safe" from the addict's probable negative response. Safe love behaviors are rarely convenient and rarely successful without a clear strategy prior to implementation. Performing safe-love behaviors provide a challenge for codependents to look for opportunities and find the courage to demonstrate these behaviors.

A safe-love behavior is something the addict can't refuse.

A safe-love behavior is most effective when the addict has difficulty refusing it. Try a hug at an appropriate time, a thoughtful note left on a pillow, a favorite breakfast served in bed, or something tangible such as clothes or even money. The principle involved here is paradoxical in nature. In other words: "Why would I give my teenage addict an extra $2.00 today (exhibiting a safe-love behavior) when only yesterday I took his paycheck away to pay for his fine (exhibiting a tough-love behavior)?" Part of the answer comes when you understand that addicts of all ages often seem to measure the amount of love given to them from others by the amount of tangible items and permissions given them. When you take things away or tell the addict "no," he or she may perceive you as rejecting and unloving. This concept will take time to understand. Again, the most important message underlying a safe-love behavior is "I love you and I have faith in your recovery but this doesn't mean I approve of what you do."

A safe-love behavior need not be face-to-face.

As noted above, safe-love behaviors must be safe for the loved-ones as well as for the addict. Typically, the addict wants love and respect from his loved ones but, because of the intensity of the disease will turn it away if the codependent were to apply the love directly. There are times in which the addict would very easily throw the safe-love behavior back in the codependent's face by arguing, calling names, or leaving the room if given the chance. One of the best safe-love behaviors is "to keep your mouth shut" instead of nagging, complaining, or persecuting. So, create a strategy wherein the addict doesn't have the chance to manipulate your safe-love behavior.

3. ACKNOWLEDGE THE ADDICT'S WORTH

A third suggestion that increases one's ability to love unconditionally is acknowledging the addict's worth. Very few substance abusers maintain any length of sobriety because their loved ones "guilt-tripped" them into sobriety. We must remind ourselves that as members of the Church, each addict has at one time or another been baptized, felt the spirit of the Holy Ghost, and has been taught about (and often still remembers) the Word of Wisdom and other moral teachings. Therefore, no gain is made by questioning the addict's worth.

Worth vs. Worthiness.

It may be helpful to make a distinction between the *worth* and the *worthiness* of an addict. Worth is the value of being a son or daughter of God. Worth is innate. Because we were born in this earth life, we are loved and acknowledged as a son or daughter of God. By that heritage alone, each of us- regardless of our worthiness-deserves respect, honor, and unconditional love as a potential God. The "worth" of any soul including the bishop's, the Relief Society president's, yours or the addict's, is great. Each of us is loved by our Heavenly Father.

On the other hand, "worthiness" may fluctuate from day to day. "Worthiness" has to do with temple recommend interviews and a level of exaltation. "Worth" has to do with being a son or daughter of God and salvation, worth is constant. As a loved one, it is most important to intervene with the addict's "worthiness" and not their "worth." As fellow brothers and sisters, we want to make sure we honor and respect the "worth" of each of our Heavenly Father's children regardless for how much they drink, steal, lie, or hurt us.

Our Eternal Potential.

The Pinegar family acknowledged the alcohol abuser's "worth." Referring to his father's alcohol use, Elder Pinegar says, "Set as your ideal the best in them that you can see." As noted by James Goodrich of the LDS Welfare Department, in the illustration below, the potential worth of addicts, even while they are "in the gutter," is the same as yours and mine.

If we are not an addict	*If we are an addict*
1. Sons and daughters of God	1. Sons and daughters of God
2. Created in God's image	2. Created in God's image
3. Given free agency	3. Given free agency
4. Placed on earth to be tested	4. Placed on earth to be tested
5. Given the Spirit of Christ	5. Given the Spirit of Christ
6. Provided with atonement for sins, based on repentance	6. Provided with atonement for sins, based on repentance
7. Resurrection of bodies	7. Resurrection of bodies
8. Rewarded according to works	8. Rewarded according to works
9. Given opportunity for eternal family	9. Given opportunity for eternal family
10. Given opportunity to become as God	10. Given opportunity to become as God

Those who misuse substances can be restored to sanity and health. Often it is difficult for us to remember that addicts are children of God too and that there is hope for their recovery. Elder Thorpe B. Isaacson, while the Presiding Bishop of the Church, said concerning those addicted to chemicals:

> They were fine before they became alcoholics (or drug addicts), and they will be fine when they are free from this habit or disease of alcoholism. They are not misfits or failures in the world. They are usually brilliant and successful, intelligent men and women. ("The Churches Responsibility in the Problem," address given at Utah School of Alcohol Studies 1956 session. © Copyright by The Church of Jesus Christ of Latter-day Saints. Used by permission.)

We must come to appreciate the fact that we are all our Father's children, part of one large family. We are sons and daughters of God who is in a very real sense the actual Father of our spirits, which gives literal significance to the phrase "Our Heavenly Father." It follows that we are all brothers and sisters, regardless of race, creed, nationality, even personal problems, whether they be addictive or codependent. There is a spark of divinity in each of us. Satan rejoices when he and his armies are able to influence us to darken *another's* divine spark by questioning, condemning, or criticizing someone else's worth and potential as one of God's children. Remember, *Faith...worketh by love* (Gal 5:6). Love is the lubricant that allows faith to work. Faith is a therapeutic tool that can change lives and invite miracles.

God has no grandchildren.

We can acknowledge the addict's worth by realizing that he or she is a direct child of God. My grandfather is a child of God. My father is a child of God. I am a child of God. My daughter is a child of God. The addict is also a child of God. We are not cousins, step-children or grandchildren. Each of us, including the addict, is a child of our Heavenly Father. As such we are loved and have special privileges.

HOLD ON WITH AN OPEN HAND
(A personal story by Dr. Rick H.)

FARM EXAMPLES

Another characteristic of unconditional love is learning how to love with an open hand. As I approached high school, my family moved to a 300-acre farm. We eventually had the horses, cows, chickens, and pigs that go along with farming. I learned a lot about people and life from the animals. For instance, one of the first horses we had got out and my older brother and I were in charge of getting it back in. As we chased the horse, we threw sticks and rocks and screamed at the horse to come back. I guess we thought we could return the horse to the pen by force. But the horse headed for the canal road, which had a cattle guard on it to prevent animals from crossing. The horse got on the canal road and headed for the cattle guard at full speed. By this time, my brother and I were left quite a ways behind the horse, but we were still throwing the rocks and the sticks. We became more intense in our pursuit as the horse got closer to the danger of the cattle guard. When we realized what was about to happen, we stopped. The horse attempted to jump the cattle guard but fell into it. Its hind legs had not cleared the guard and its hoofs were trapped between the metal railings. We spent the next few hours freeing the injured horse.

Since that incident, I've wondered if my brother and I were responsible for the injuries of the horse because of the nature of our pursuit. Of course, we were only trying to help him, but would the horse have fallen into the cattle guard had we not been exhibiting persecuting behaviors such as throwing rocks and sticks? I later learned the correct way to catch a horse. First, get a bucket of oats and place some of the oats in your open hand. Then call the horse's name and let the oats fall from your open hand into the bucket. With this gentile coaxing, the horse will eventually return on its own.

The small chicks taught me a similar lesson. We would buy fifty or so chicks each spring and place them in the chicken coop with a heat light. Of course, I liked to go in and play with them. I would chase them into a corner and catch one of them. As long as I held my hand tightly around the chick, it would remain in my hand. I later learned I could simply hold open my hand under the heat lamp and the chicks would pile onto my hand. No restraint at all was needed.

The horse and the chicks taught me a very important attribute of God's love. *Hold on to what you love with an open hand*. Many of us believe that the love we have for someone is measured best by how tight we hold on to them or how much anger and frustration we show when they disappoint us. Let's examine the Lord's approach. At what point does the Lord close his hand and say we are not welcome? One might ask, "How much sin does it take for *God* to stop loving you?" These seem like very silly questions to even be asking. Of course God's hand is always open. Of course we are always welcome. Remember, the Iron Rod referred to in Lehi's dream does not have a chain-link fence around it. Each of us may let go of it and explore the spacious building and wander through the mist and return to the Iron Rod. This all happens with God's open hand waiting for our return.

Replacing persecuting behaviors with unconditional love, or at least safe-love behaviors, is essential in continuing the recovery process. This unconditional love should be similar to the love exhibited by the good Samaritan to the injured man. We must overlook our natural instincts to view the addict as our "enemy." We must ask ourselves, "Is our love of the addict stronger than the cords of death?"

Now let's finish the story of the good Samaritan. After the Samaritan was assured that the injured man's life was preserved, he did a very important thing: "...he departed..." and went on to Jerusalem (If we are to assume that he was traveling from Jericho to Jerusalem). The good Samaritan did not cancel his trip and take the injured person home to Jericho. He simply postponed it to demonstrate unconditional love toward the "enemy." Had the good Samaritan been codependent, he likely would never have completed his trip to Jerusalem.

This act of moving on introduces us to the next attribute of love. A third attribute of Christ-like love is tough love. Tough love suggests that loved ones have a destination in their hearts *personal salvation* and the courage to seek that destination and go on with their journey as the Good Samaritan did.

SUMMARY

Love Attribute #2.

Hold on to what you love with an open hand just like God holds on to us.

Scripture.

But a certain Samaritan, as he journeyed, came where he was: and when he saw him, *he had compassion on him*, And went to him, and bound up his wounds, pouring in oil and wine, and set him on his own beast, and brought him to an inn, *and took care of him*. And on the morrow... *he departed*... (Luke 10:33-35, *emphasis added*)

LET GO

To "let go" does not mean to stop caring,
   it means I can't do it for someone else;
To "let go" is not to cut myself off,
   it's the realization that I can't control another;
To "let go" is not to enable,
   but to allow learning from natural consequences;
To "let go" is to admit powerlessness
   which means the outcome is not in my hands;
To "let go" is not to try to change or blame another,
   it's to make the most of myself;
To "let go" is not to "care for,"
   but to "care about;"
To "let go" is not to judge,
   but to allow another to be a human being;
To "let go" is to not be in the middle, arranging all the outcomes,
   but to allow others to affect their own destinies;
To "let go" is not to be protective,
   it's to permit another to face reality;
To "let go" is not to deny,
   but to accept;
To "let go" is not to nag, scold, or argue,
   but instead to search out my own shortcomings and correct them;
To "let go" is not to adjust everything to my desires,
   but to take each day as it comes, and cherish myself in it;
To "let go" is not to criticize and regulate anybody,
   but to try to become what I dream I can be;
To "let go" is to not regret the past,
   but to grow and live for the future;
To "let go" is to fear less and love more.

CHAPTER EIGHT

TOUGH LOVE
ALLOW THE REFINING FIRE TO BURN

Tough love is the third attribute of God's kind of love. As discussed in Chapter Three surrounding loved ones often find themselves performing "rescuing behaviors" in an attempt to cure the addict. These behaviors save the addict from the immediate consequences of his or her own substance use and include enabling, covering up, denying, and lying. The end result of such behaviors for the addict is further loss of self-worth and continued substance use. Behind each irresponsible addict, there is a "too responsible" codependent. Behind each irresponsible addict husband is a hyper-responsible wife, boss, bishop or other individual. Elder John K. Carmack, while addressing the third annual conference of S.A.V.E., stated the following:

> I've learned a lot of things from my brothers and uncles who have suffered from alcoholism....You need to be both loving and tough....You have to be strong enough not to give too much, but kind enough to help. At times it is hard to say "No." An alcoholic will show anger, use ridicule, try to shame you and attempt to make you feel guilty, but you have to be strong to deal effectively with the alcoholic [drug addict]....Very often the alcoholic [drug addict] must reach a low level in his life before anyone can help. He must also experience much pain before getting to that level...If alcoholics [and drug addicts] live long enough, life will teach them "by the things which they suffer." (*By The Things Which They Suffer*, S.A.V.E., 1988)

Typically, addicts will seek help *not* when the problem is pointed out or as treatment is recommended, but when their pain motivates them to act. A general guideline for those wishing to be helpful is: *Do nothing to alleviate the pain of an addict.* Of course, as members of the LDS Church, we might perceive the exact opposite to be true: Do everything you possibly can to alleviate the pain of everyone, including an addict. Such a philosophy presents a unique problem for members of the LDS Church in effectively performing tough love behaviors. Many LDS persons believe it is wrong and sinful to allow loved ones to hurt or suffer even if their pain is in consequence to their own irresponsible behavior. It is difficult for LDS codependents to believe in their hearts that it is better for addicts to pass through sorrow so that they can learn.

In the *Resource Manual for Helping Families with Alcohol Problems*, the following suggestions are recommended by the LDS Church:

> Love is often difficult to show, especially when it results in pain. When someone we love abuses alcohol or other drugs that are harmful, our tendency is to help him out of his problems because we love him....The problem drinker [and drug user] must experience for himself the consequences of his drinking [or drug use]....The object is not to be vengeful, but rather to motivate him to receive the help he needs to overcome his problem. By showing "tough love," we do what is best for him. Circumstances and inescapable choices motivate change. Threats only cause a problem drinker [or drug user] to make promises that he seldom keeps. (*Resource Manual for Helping Families with Alcohol Problems*, PGSC6258 LDS Church, 1984 p. 99. © Copyright by The Church of Jesus Christ of Latter-day Saints. Used by permission.)

THE PRODIGAL SON

The good Samaritan discussed in Luke 10:33-35, and the prodigal son discussed in Luke 15:11-32 teach us two attributes of God's kind of love. We discussed the parable of the good Samaritan in Chapter Seven on unconditional love to illustrate the concept of "loving thy enemy." The good Samaritan "departed" and went on to Jerusalem after he demonstrated that love. The prodigal son teaches another aspect of love. The parable begins with a father and his two sons.

> And the younger of them said to his father, Father give me the portion of goods that falleth to me, and he divided unto him his living. And not many days after the younger son gathered all together, and took his journey into a far county, and there wasted his substance with riotous living. And when he had spent all, there arose a mighty famine in that land and he began to be in want...And he would fain have filled his belly with the husks that the swine did eat: *and no man gave unto him*. (Luke 15:13, 14 & 16, *emphasis added*)

Interestingly enough, few readers hold the father responsible for his son's behavior, even though it was he who gave him the "the portion of the goods." Neither do we read of the father anguishing over the decision to do so. We simply read that the father gave the prodigal his portion and then hear no more about the father until the son returns home. The father had sufficient self love so he respected his son's free agency, and was able to give him his fortune "with an open hand." If the father had been codependent he would have worried excessively about giving his son the money or about what his son was doing while he "took his journey." This worry could have caused the father physical illness, or he might have left his duties at home in pursuit of his son and, in doing so, lost his own fortune.

The parable of the prodigal son illustrates that unlike the parable of the good Samaritan "no man gave unto" the son. This teaches the concept of tough love, which is, there is a time and place for loved ones "not to give," Immediately after the words "and no man gave unto him," come the words "And when he came to himself." This phrase suggests that the son "hit bottom" as a result of tough love, and eventually "came home." Additionally, upon the prodigal son's return, the father demonstrated unconditional love "...his father saw him, and had compassion, and ran, and fell on his neck, and kissed him" (Luke 15:20).

Learning from Parables.

To apply the "take care of him" attitude toward the prodigal son would likely promote failure and a repetition of his irresponsible behavior. The Samaritan helped a man in crisis who had been beaten and robbed. Through no apparent fault of his own, the man became a victim of aggressive violence.

The prodigal son chose and carried out his "riotous living," and no one came to his rescue. He was experiencing more than a crisis and required a change of heart. The essential element in the prodigal son story is that the father demonstrated tough love, believing that if his son was not pampered and protected, the normal consequences of life would teach him and cause spiritual growth to occur. It worked.

Would the prodigal son have changed his life if the good Samaritan had been traveling by while he was eating husks with the swine? What if the good Samaritan had taken care of the son in the same way he took care of the injured Jew? Would the prodigal son have "[come] unto himself?" I believe the non-codependent good Samaritan would probably have discerned the difference and realized greater love for the boy would be demonstrated by passing him by.

Some Church and family members may contribute to the addict's problem because they believe one must always play the role of the good Samaritan. Many addicts are killed by kindness. That is, loved ones apply the principle of the good Samaritan when what is needed is the principle of tough love found in the parable of the prodigal son.

THE REFINER'S FIRE

There are different types of suffering. Some suffering is secondary to sin, some secondary to breaking natural laws, and some secondary to righteousness. Pain, trials and tribulations must occur in our lives and in the lives of our loved ones if we are to be sufficiently refined to return to our Heavenly Father.

Joseph in Prison.
"Oh God, where art thou?" was Joseph Smith's plea while he was imprisoned in Liberty Jail in 1838-39. The Lord's answer also sheds light on the benefits of suffering. While Joseph was in jail, the Saints were being persecuted, robbed, and murdered, and among the Saints there was dissension and apostasy. Perhaps more painful than the coldness of the jail was Joseph's discouragement. Joseph's pain might have been intensified because of his perfect knowledge that the Lord

could have freed him. Certainly he remembered the visits from Moroni, John the Baptist, Peter, James, John, and a host of other heavenly messengers including Heavenly Father and Jesus Christ. It was in this setting that Joseph cried, "O God, where art thou? And where is the pavilion that covereth thy hiding place?" (D&C 121:1) To this plea came the Lord's answer: "My son, peace be unto thy soul; thine adversity and thine afflictions shall be but a small moment." (D&C 121:7) Referring to the pain and suffering, Christ said to Joseph, "Know thou, my son, that all these things shall give thee experience, and shall be for thy good" (D&C 122:7).

Christ loved Joseph Smith enough to allow him to remain and suffer in prison, and thereby gain "experience." It is very difficult to allow a loved one to suffer when one has the power to alleviate the pain, hence, the term "tough love."

A similar cry to Joseph's comes from codependents "O God, where art thou?" Surrounding family members might think that God has truly forsaken them and their loved one the addict. God could have freed the codependent from such an enormous amount of suffering and pain, yet He did not. How quickly we forget that there is great purpose behind our life struggles. Out of frustration, loved ones begin to free the addict from the pain, hoping it will also alleviate their own pain. By so doing these codependents innocently rescue the addict from the very thing that will be for "[their] good."

After the Lord told Joseph, "These things shall give thee experience, and shall be for thy good," He said, "The Son of Man hath descended below them all. Art thou greater than he?" (D&C 122:8.) Bishop Glenn L. Pace, second counselor in the Presiding Bishopric, discusses this very topic, suggesting that part of the reason the Savior suffered in the Gethsemane was so that he would have infinite compassion for us as we experience our trials and tribulations including those associated with the misuse of substances. Through His suffering, the Savior became qualified to be the perfect judge. Not one of us will be able to approach him on Judgment Day and say, "You don't know what it was like having a addict in your home!" Indeed, He knows the nature of our trials better than we do, for He "descended below them all." (*Ensign*, Sept., 1988 p. 71.)

Garden of Gethsemane.

As a loving Father and Mother in Heaven viewed their beloved son suffering in the Garden of Gethsemane, the Savior cried out,

> O my Father if it be possible, let this cup pass from me: nevertheless not as I will but as thou wilt. (Matt. 26:39)

It appears that the "will" of Heavenly Father and Mother was to allow Christ to suffer. Even the Son of God was not allowed to forgo the "bitter cup." Can you imagine the tears in the eyes of the Father and our sweet Heavenly Mother when they had to deny their son's request? Can we comprehend the sacred tears shed by them when they had to abandon the Savior on the cross and hear him say, "My God, my God, why hast thou forsaken me?" (Mark 15:34) It is interesting to note, that even though Heavenly Father and Mother withdrew their spirit for a brief time (this would be considered tough love), an angel was sent (Luke 22:43) in response to Christ's pain (this would be considered safe love).

Other examples.

The refiner's fire has been lit and it appears that "Even the son learned obedience by the things which he suffered" (Hebrews 5:8). If the Son of God had to learn "obedience" by the things which he suffered, how is it that an addict will learn obedience to the Word of Wisdom or the Law of Chastity in any other fashion but by suffering? Many scriptural examples support this idea.

In 2 Nephi 2:11 we read,

> For it must needs be, that there is an opposition in all things. If not so...righteousness could not be brought to pass, neither wickedness, neither holiness nor misery, neither good nor bad.

And in D&C 95:1: "..and whom I love I also chasten..." And the concept is very clearly taught in Helaman 15:3: "...yea, in the days of their iniquities hath he chastened them because he loveth them." Even nonscriptural references can teach this principle. Benjamin Franklin is known to have said, "Those things that hurt, instruct."

These illustrations teach us that there is a celestial form of tough love. Love so strong that it withstands the "refiner's fire." The Lord will allow those He loves the most to suffer because He has faith in them and wants them to return to Him in exaltation with all power and glory. He applies the principle taught by the prodigal son to our lives. For loved ones it truly takes great spirituality to introduce pain into the lives of an addict with love.

The addict's suffering is one of two essential ingredients of recovery from addiction. The other element is a spiritual awakening. Codependents who can facilitate the addict's experience with pain assist in the addict's recovery. But, codependents are generally powerless over the spiritually awakening component of the addict's recovery. As discussed in Chapter One, a spiritual experience must occur if true recovery is to take place. The formula for the addict in recovery may be depicted as seen below:

SUFFERING + SPIRITUAL AWAKENING = RECOVERY

Addiction is a unique disease requiring a unique intervention. In order to get well, an addict must hit bottom, feel pain and be allowed to suffer. And if it appears that the "refiner's fire" is not hot enough and the addict is not suffering, simply "throw more wood on." Suffering is the only instrument sharp enough to prune away the excesses of the addict's will and to fashion it into a reasonable facsimile of God's will. The task for the codependent, once God has lit the refining fire, is to let it burn and, as needed, throw a few pieces of wood on and not follow their natural inclination of "grabbing a fire extinguisher" and putting out the fire.

HOW DOES ONE DEVELOP TOUGH-LOVE?

1. ADMIT YOUR POWERLESSNESS

Powerless over the things God "would not" do.
There are at least two areas in which codependents must accept that they are powerless. Elder Richard G. Scott in the May 1988 *Ensign* article entitled "To Help a Loved One In Need" identifies these two areas. He explains the first one as, "Do not attempt to override agency." Certainly God has the *power* to take away free agency. Satan's plan, "sought to destroy the agency of man, which...the Lord God had *given* him" (Moses 4:3, *emphasis added*). By refusing Satan's plan in the pre-existence God demonstrated that He chooses not to override one's free agency.

Many codependents have spent a great portion of their lives trying to manage their addict's behavior, by insisting they stop drinking, using drugs, or acting out sexually. But this is hopeless. Brigham Young said,

> A great many [parents, spouses, and loved ones] think that they will be able to flog people into heaven, but this can never be done, for the intelligence in us is as independent as the Gods. People are not to be driven and you can put into a gnat's eye all the souls of the children of men that are driven into heaven by preaching hellfire. (President Brigham Young, *Discourses of Brigham Young.* p. 64. © Copyright by The Church of Jesus Christ of Latter-day Saints. Used by permission.)

The interpersonal relationships of faithful Church members are undermined, damaged, and destroyed by well-meaning attempts of those who try to force another to live by righteous principles. A happy, mutually satisfying relationship will not long survive tactics of control, regardless of the reason. *Some people can get very ugly in the name of righteousness*. They sometimes violate gospel principles in a much more offensive way than the addict they are trying to correct. A successful, eternal relationship must be built slowly and carefully on a foundation of individual agency. The codependent who wishes to demonstrate tough love must accept his or her own powerlessness over the addict's free agency. We want to treat addicts the same way God treats us-by teaching them correct principles, by facilitating justice, and respecting their response to those "just" consequences, be it hunger, jail, sadness, anger, and even death.

Powerless over the things only God can do.

The second area where Elder Scott says we are powerless is in the things only God can do. While there are some things codependents can do to help the addict, there are some things that can only be done by God. The spiritual awakening that each addict must experience during the course of his or her recovery can only be achieved as God (or the Holy Ghost) intervenes in the life of the addict. Certainly codependents may preach, invite, encourage and pray for the addict, but *only God can send the angel* and only the Holy Ghost can cause the addict's testimony "to burn."

The story of Alma the Younger and the four sons of Mosiah (Mosiah 27:8-15) affirms this concept. Alma the Younger and the four sons of Mosiah were "unbelievers," preaching against the Church. Verse 11 states "The angel of the Lord appears" unto Alma and the sons of Mosiah. Here a spiritual awakening begins. It's interesting to note whose angel appeared. Though in verse 14, we learn the angel was sent partly because of loved ones' prayers the angel belonged to the Lord. It was the Lord's angel, not Alma's angel. Simply speaking, codependents are responsible for exhibiting those behaviors that remain after they peacefully admit they are powerless over the things only God can do (like send an angel or override the addict's free agency).

2. DEMONSTRATE FAITH IN THE ADDICT

Faith in the addict is essential in performing effective tough love. It takes a lot of faith in addicts to believe that they can successfully cope with the future suffering that might await them, such as lost homes, money problems, and incarceration. The majority of addicts are not stupid or retarded. In fact, many of them are very bright and each is a child of God with a great potential, the potential to survive the pain that will surely come during the disease of addiction and recovery. God is faithful we will overcome temptation (1 Cor. 10:13). So, we too should have faith in the addict and his or her ability to overcome tribulation. D&C 121:44 reads, "That he may know that thy faithfulness is stronger than the cords of death." This suggests that we should demonstrate our love and faithfulness in the addict who has strayed "beyond the cords of death."

Understandingly, it is difficult to remember that a fifteen-year-old addict who can't even get out of bed, who rarely attends school, and who is creating so many problems is a child of God and has eternal potential. But it is true. If given the chance, most addicts can survive and grow from their suffering. Each and every promise given in the addict's patriarchal blessing is potentially possible.

Sin of unfaithfulness.

Inability to perform tough love is a sin of *unfaithfulness* inability to turn an addict over to God's care demonstrates a lack of faith in God to perform miracles and also demonstrates a lack of faith in the individual who has gone astray. A codependent questions the addict's worth as a child of God. Unless the addict is truly handicapped, he or she can live without you and can return to Heavenly Father without you but not without God. Codependents should try to love addicts enough to allow them to experience the consequences of their own sinful behaviors or allow God's tough love to be demonstrated in their lives. Unless we exercise sufficient faith in God, we deny Him the opportunity to help us and the addict. As faith and spirituality increase so does hope for recovery. "The Lord is able to do all things according to his will for the children of men, if it so be that they exercise faith in him" (1 Nephi 7:12).

3. ADMINISTER THE LAW OF MOSES

The Lord gave Moses the higher priesthood and revealed the fullness of the gospel. But Children of Israel rebelled and manifested such gross unworthiness that God took from them the power whereby they could have become a kingdom of priests and of kings. He gave them instead a lesser law, a law of carnal commandments, a preparatory gospel, a schoolmaster to bring them to Christ and the fullness of His gospel. He gave them what is known as the Law of Moses. At that time the Israelites' ability to be governed by a higher law or hold a higher priesthood was limited. The Lord, in response to the Israelites' level of righteousness, dealt with them accordingly. Addicts, while in the active phase of using, are like the Israelites wandering in the wilderness. Therefore, codependents should deal with them in a manner equal to their reduced level of spirituality. Many codependents become deeply frustrated when they expect addicts to live a higher spiritual law and insist they go to church, pray daily, read the scriptures and so forth, when in reality most addicts have trouble just being in compliance with a lesser law. That is, most addicts have difficulty with even the simplest laws, such as not stealing, telling the truth, staying out of jail, and not hurting others.

Characteristics of the Law of Moses that might be helpful in developing a strategy of tough love include:

1. Clear and precise consequences attached to each misbehavior. (Exodus 21:23-25)
2. Swift and unmitigated justice.
3. Very limited mercy.
4. "Double payment" demanded often from the sinner, as was sometimes the practice under the Law of Moses. (Exodus 22:3-4)

Consequences and Justice.

According to the Law of Justice it is believed that each offense/sin will require a payment. Some of the most effective interventions into the lives of addicts have been when a *double* portion was required of the addict to be restored prior to return of full freedom. If $10 was stolen $20 was expected in return. My explanation for such a requirement would be: "You owe me $10 because that was the amount you took and you owe $10 more for the behavior of stealing and lying about it." The power of requiring a *double* portion immediately demonstrates to the addict your sincerity as well as your faith in their potential to overcome problems.

Again such procedures are not suggested for everyone, no more than God would have dealt with all his children during all the dispensations of time with the Law of Moses and the lesser priesthood. Rather, such an approach seems to be very effective for intervening with those on the lower end of the spirituality continuum. By utilizing principles from the Law of Moses codependents can assist the substance abusers to advance where the Spirit of the Lord and the higher law might eventually be received.

WHAT TOUGH LOVE IS NOT

Withholding love is not Tough Love.

The withholding of mercy and love from the addict by the family members is at times viewed as tough love and used as an intervention strategy. There is no doubt that it is much easier to withdraw love and to perform what appears to be tough-love behaviors out of anger, resentment, and bitterness in an attempt to punish the addict for his or her wrong doings. Codependents often react to the addict's illness with anger, hatred, resentment, and suffering and detach from their personal feelings and love because their pain becomes so intense. *To withhold love, respect, and hope from the addict prevents the Spirit of Christ from working in your behalf and further evidences the depths to which you have fallen into codependency!* Tough love, when performed correctly, stems from an INCREASE of love, faith, and respect for the addict and not from a DECREASE. Tough love is a manifestation of the Pure Love of Christ. It is the same love that allowed the Prodigal's father to go on with his life while the Prodigal was doing his "riotous living". The same love that Heavenly Father and Mother demonstrated when they left Their beloved Son alone in the Garden of Gethsemane and on the cross.

Guilt trips are not part tough love.

In the following paragraph Elder Dean L. Larsen gives an excellent example of how guilt can be a wrong intervention.

> Peace of mind comes when we know we are doing the right things for the right reasons. For some reason one of the most common methods many of us use to motivate is to develop feelings of guilt within ourselves or in others for whom we have a responsibility. Guilt feelings are a natural product of an injured conscience. When we willfully violate a valid code of conduct, we suffer the consequences of our infraction in the internal conflict that occurs within our souls. Such feelings, painful and remorseful though they may be, can generate the desire to repent and improve. They can be useful, constructive emotions that propel us forward to greater perfection. *But purposefully generating feelings of guilt over some shortcomings as a means of motivating action or promoting more compliant behavior is rarely productive.* The devastating effect of a child's constantly being told that he is stupid, lazy or ugly has been well documented in behavioral studies. When anyone's honest effort to do better or to be better is met by debilitating criticism, real motivation and incentive are often destroyed. But we must be helped to feel that we are valued and appreciated in spite of our shortcomings. ("The Peaceable Things of the Kingdom," Feb. 1986, *The New ERA*, p. 8, *emphasis added*. © Copyright by The Church of Jesus Christ of Latter-day Saints. Used by permission.)

WHAT TOUGH LOVE IS

Tough love allows loved ones to give responsibilities to the addict and allows them to confront the addict if and when those responsibilities are not met. Tough love necessarily creates a crisis that facilitates negative consequences for the substance-using behaviors. Tough love is firm, confident, easily understood, founded upon the Law of Moses (or Justice), and it seeks an increase in the codependent's spirituality. When implementing tough love, loved ones should be consistent, predictable, and dependable. And developing strategies they should be inventive, creative, and responsible.

BITE, DON'T BARK

Several years ago I counseled a young man named Tom who suffered with a drinking problem. I worked with him off and on for about two years. Tom's parents were as sweet, loving, and as spiritual as any I have ever met and they truly wanted to help their son. As their counselor, I intervened, using traditional methods like personal and family counseling. Though I worked closely with the parents, we experienced very little success. Regardless of our efforts, Tom would end up in the local jail several times a month for public intoxication. After each incident Tom's parents rushed to bail him out and then brought him to my office the following Monday.

After this cycle went on for several months, the parents and I decided that the next time Tom was arrested we would leave him in jail. This was a difficult decision, because just a few months earlier a young man jailed in a neighboring state had been killed by inmates. We considered the possibility of this happening to Tom, we had no other choice. After more than a dozen public intoxication charges, something needed to be done because Tom was risking his life anyway through his excessive use of alcohol.

Eventually Tom gained ability to maintain his sobriety. In sharing one of the turning points in his life, he relates:

> My mom and dad would always preach to me about why I shouldn't drink. They would try guilt trips, get the bishop to talk to me, threaten me, try to bribe me. They tried everything. All they did was bark just like a dog. It wasn't until they started to bite that I began to pay attention. All the barking in the world couldn't teach me as much as sitting in jail that first night.

Often parents and loved ones believe that their most useful tool for intervention is *talking*. That is, they believe the addict will learn by listening to their carefully prepared speeches, as if the addict were a normal, healthy, and functional person. Unfortunately, it appears that part of the disease of addiction is a hardening of the addict's heart and turning off of the ears. The *least* effective intervention strategy during the later stages of addiction seems to be "talking." Tough love behaviors have proven much more effective.

Many fears and traditions make it difficult to feel the freedom that will come by loving as God loves. By accepting the challenge to show tough love, you could change a life for all eternity. The importance of exhibiting tough love and demonstrating faith in the addict is best illustrated in this poem.

> Come to the edge.
> No, we will fall.
>
> Come to the edge.
> No, we will fall.
>
> They came to the edge.
> He pushed them, and they flew.

The chart on the following page is an illustration of recovery stages for LDS codependents as discussed in the previous three chapters. Now is the time to bring the three attributes of God together and demonstrate God's kind of love.

SUMMARY

Love Attribute #3
Allow God's refining fire to burn and if the fire isn't hot enough, throw some more wood on.

Scripture
...And [he] took his journey into a far country, and there wasted his substance with riotous living. And when he had spent all, there arose a mighty famine in that land and he began to be in want...And he would fain have filled his belly with the husks that the swine did eat: *and no man gave unto him*. (Luke 15:13, 14 & 16, *emphasis added*)

The LDS Family Recovering from Codependence

Tough Love

Increase Faith In Addict
Detach From Addict's Behavior
Cease Covering-Up
Use Strategies Prayerfully
Feel Less Responsible For Addict

Unconditional Love

Increase Spirituality
Receive Divine Intervention
Forgive Self and Addict
Acknowledge Addict's Worth
Perform Safe-Love Behaviors
Accept "Disease" Model

Self-Love

Identify Resources
Spend Time Alone
Take Care of Personal Needs
Do "Sunbeam Check"
Set Priorities
Recognize Codependent Role

Self-Reliance

Bottom

CHAPTER NINE

BRINGING IT TOGETHER
GOD'S KIND OF LOVE

There is a book entitled *All I Really Need to Know I Learned in Kindergarten*, by Robert Fulghum. If there were an LDS version of this book, it would be, *All I really need to know I learned in Primary*. Or, *Much of what I need to know to make it into the Celestial Kingdom I learned in Primary*. The 12-step groups have a saying. It is "keep it simple." This chapter brings together the three attributes of God's kind of love in a simple understandable fashion.

STRATEGIES

By now you have some understanding of addiction, codependence and the three attributes of God's kind of love. Lets bring these various attributes of love together and establish a plan of how to relate to the addict "just for today."

A reader of the Book of Mormon might ask, "Why did Mormom use so much valuable space on the gold plates to record military action and battle strategy?" One explanation might be that the war stories contain useful information about how Satan and his forces operate. The record also describes inspired strategies for defending ourselves against this evil. Seemingly insignificant military details reveal valuable advice when one recognizes that the stories apply to the war against evil today. (Kathleen S. McConkie, "Defending Against Evil," *Ensign*, Jan 1992, p. 19.)

In Alma 43:30, Captain Moroni and his generals are fighting Zerahemnah and the Lamanite army. In this scripture, Moroni talks about the appropriate use of "stratagem" in defending the Nephites.

> And he [Moroni] also knowing that it was the only desire of the Nephites to preserve their lands, and their liberty, and their church, therefore he thought it no sin that he should defend them by *stratagem...* (*emphasis added*)

This scripture states that under particular circumstances, the use of "stratagem" might be an appropriate measure acceptable to our Heavenly Father in defending certain rights. Moroni identifies the circumstances for the appropriate use of stratagem, that is in the preserving of land, liberty, and church. Countless examples show how Satan's use of addiction can literally destroy any and all of these. A few stories are shared below.

LANDS

An LDS woman, married fifteen years, called her counselor for an emergency appointment. At the very moment of this appointment her husband was at home drunk and their home and property were being repossessed. Horrified at the prospect of losing "everything," she shared her husband's progress through the various stages of alcoholism over the years. First, he had been self-employed and lost their business. Financial problems and alcohol use ensued. Eventually, she had to find a job to support the family while he "sat home and drank." Unable to financially care for their three children and pay all the bills, she fell behind on the house payment. All the while, for the past several months her husband had been unemployed, at home, and drinking. As she discussed the situation, it was painfully obvious that any intervention was too late. Alcohol had robbed this good sister of her home, her property, her "lands".

LIBERTY

A single LDS parent shares her personal experiences. With tears in her eyes she shows a ring of a dozen or more keys. She relates the anguish caused by her teenage son, who has been abusing drugs and alcohol for nearly three years. Over the months she has resorted to putting everything of value under lock and key within her own home. She describes how her home has locks on every door, how she has to constantly be careful about leaving her purse unguarded. Her son steals from her to get money for drugs and alcohol. At the very moment she is relating this story, she expresses a fear about what her son might be doing at home. She worries: "Will he pick the lock on my bedroom door again?" "Will he find the tithing money?" Even while she sleeps she is frightened that her son will sneak in and take money from the purse she hides beneath her pillow. For months she claims *no relief from the fear*. Many times she remains at the house to guard her home and property when she really wants to be somewhere else. Alcohol and drugs have robbed this good mother of her personal freedom and "liberty."

CHURCH

A brother who has served as a bishop twice, as a high councilor, and as a professional counselor shares his story. This faithful man tells how he was "twisted" because of feelings associated with his teenage son's sexual addiction. At times the guilt, the worries, the emotional strain of having a teenage sex addict would interfere with his spiritual activities. His son's addiction interfered with his father going to the temple, teaching priesthood classes, and maintaining family togetherness. In a very direct way, the father often felt unworthy to perform Church callings because of the shame and guilt of having an addict as a son. He had allowed his son's pornography use to directly interfere with his own personal church and spiritual growth.

As Moroni defended the Nephites with the use of stratagem, codependents must be willing to use stratagem to preserve their lands, liberty, and church against destruction brought on by addiction. The battle against one of Satan's greatest tools, addiction, will not be won with half-hearted efforts.

HOW DOES ONE DEVELOP STRATEGIES?

1. DETACHING IS ESSENTIAL

Detaching from the chaos and negative emotions of an addict is essential in developing a strategy. The key to "detaching" from the addict is to "attach" oneself to a higher power. Getting angry and being resentful about someone else's behavior ought to remind us that *this isn't between the addict and me but, rather between God and me*. If your spouse eats more sweets than you would like, if your son is more sexually active than you would prefer, and if anger results and you yell and scream and threaten, then codependency occurs and powerlessness sets in. You have now committed a sin. Your behavior-temper, lack of patience, inability to love your enemy-is for God and you to resolve.

Sin against God and Heavens.
The key to detaching is to realize those codependent behaviors of rescuing, persecuting, and suffering are between you and God, *not* between you and the addict. Whether it appears you are offending the addict or someone else is not the most important issue. Your misbehaviors are between you and God. The following are some scriptural examples of how sin is a *personal* issue.

> And it came to pass after these things, that his master's wife cast her eyes upon Joseph; and she said, Lie with me. But he refused, and said unto his master's wife, Behold, my master wotteth not what is with me in the house, and he hath committed all that he hath to my hand; There is none greater in this house than I; neither hath he kept back any thing from me but thee. Because thou art his wife; *how then can I do this great wickedness, and sin against God?* (Genesis 39:7 & 8, *emphasis added*)

You would think that Joseph would be offending Potiphar or Potiphar's wife if he had had an affair. But the scripture suggests that Joseph was most concerned about what the sin would do to his relationship with his God. Joseph wasn't worried about earthly consequences, i.e., going to prison. He knew the greater punishment would come from God and was able to apply "Principle before Personality." That is, because of his relationship with God, he placed the principle of honesty and integrity above the personalty of Potiphar and his wife.

This brings us to a final discussion of the prodigal son. After all his "riotous living," and after he "came to himself," who was the prodigal son worried about offending? During that long journey home to his father, what could have been going on in the son's mind. One might think the great offense was against his father and his family. But the son says,

> I will arise and go to my father, and will say unto him, Father, I have *sinned against heaven*... (Luke 15:18, *emphasis added*.)

Again it is clear that when we transgress we sin "against heaven." We should as the prodigal son, evaluate our behaviors against heaven and God. This concept of "the problem being between you and God" allows the codependent to detach from the binding cords of codependence and focus on what matters most following Christ. Placing Christ at the center of our lives brings proper perspective to our relationships. Viewing our behaviors as they offend or please Christ is a key to changing that perspective. A couple of scriptural examples emphasize the importance of being "Christ-dependent" and not "Others-dependent."

> And whatsoever ye do, do it heartily, as to the Lord, and not unto men; Knowing that of the Lord ye shall receive the reward of the inheritance for ye serve the Lord Christ. (Colossians 3: 23 and 24)

> And another of his disciples said unto him, Lord, suffer me first to go and bury my father. But Jesus said unto him, Follow me; and let the dead bury their dead. (Matthew 8:20, 21)

The primary reason for our existence is to follow Christ. If certain behaviors prevent us from walking on our own two feet back to our Heavenly Father, then codependency has occurred and needs to be resolved. Detaching from the addict is extremely difficult to do, especially if he or she has just embarrassed you, hurt you, or stole from you. But keep in mind that what is truly of importance to your salvation is what you do as a result of the addict's behavior. *Codependents can measure the level of their recovery by determining their ability to act and feel according to their relationship with God regardless of the addict's behavior.* Achieving some level of detachment allows the codependent to add the additional ingredients of an effective strategy.

2. HOLD FREQUENT STRATEGY SESSIONS

Holding frequent strategy sessions is essential to developing strategies. Once a certain level of detachment is obtained, the "generals" must meet to make a plan. For Moroni, the plan was developed and executed by himself, his Heavenly Father, generals and soldiers. Part of his plan included where to hide his armies and how to trap the enemy. For codependents, the plan should be developed by those "selected generals" who surround the addict. Codependents need to identify which "generals" should be involved in the strategy sessions. One should invite only those who will be effective generals to the strategy meetings.

A successful strategy includes the demonstration of the three attributes of love, namely self-love, unconditional love and tough love. These attributes may be viewed as essential tools necessary to fight a battle as powerful as addiction. Certainly a general would prefer to have the Army, the Navy and the Air Force on his or her side if at all possible. In a similar fashion, the codependent needs access to all three attributes of love.

3. BALANCE TOUGH LOVE AND UNCONDITIONAL LOVE

Assuming the generals have been identified and detachment has occurred, the strategy begins by having loved ones effectively balance intervention behaviors with *tough love* and *unconditional love*. Tough love and unconditional love are eternal principles that need to be carefully balanced on the principle of self-love. The disciplinary activity of tough love must take place within the framework of unconditional love. Doing this is often difficult for codependents because they view these roles as contradictory. An illustration showing how tough love and unconditional love work together appears on the following page.

D&C 121:43 suggests that we should not only unconditionally love our enemies but, we should actually demonstrate an "increase of love" toward them after they have offended us.

> Reproving betimes with sharpness, when moved upon by the Holy Ghost; and then showing forth afterwards an increase of love toward him whom thou hast reproved lest he esteem thee to be his enemy. (D&C 121:43)

As introduced in this scripture, there are at least two ways to have "power and influence" over another. The first, is by "reproving betimes with sharpness," which could be interpreted as using tough love. The second way is by showing an "increase of love," which is exhibiting unconditional love. One method alone typically does *not* produce change. The Lord used the word "and," not "or," when instructing us in the scripture. Each type of love is essential in making a successful strategy for change.

Some codependents do a terrific job "reproving," or showing tough love. Some have even attended nationally organized Tough-Love support groups. One LDS couple had attended some Tough-Love groups and then emptied their teen's room of clothes, bed and stereo for breaking agreements made in behavior-change contracts. These parents were left feeling desperate because their teen was still "delinquent." They had nothing left to take away, and nothing had worked. In fact, the mother was very concerned because her son was now throwing a dart at her picture on his empty bedroom door. In essence, the teen "esteemed the parents to be enemies," in part because they neglected to show the "increase of love" with their toughness. The prophet Brigham Young once counseled, "Never chasten beyond the balm you have within you to bind up." (*Journal of Discourses*, 9:124-25)

God-Like Love

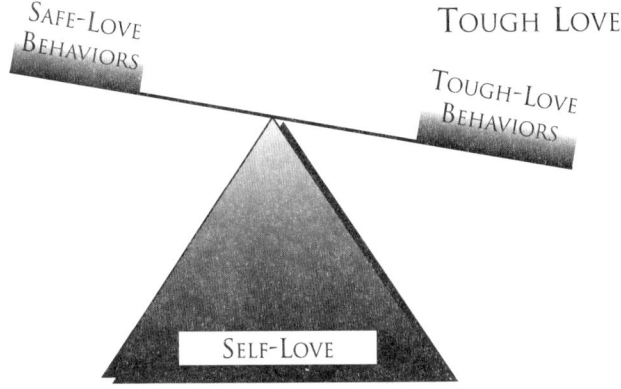

As you develop your strategy, carefully think through every possibility, including both tough-love and safe-love behaviors. As discussed in Chapter Seven, safe love is one behavior most of us will begin to exhibit. At this point the codependent is healthier than the addict and more willing to act. Therefore, it makes good sense for codependents to make certain that critical decisions rather than wait and hope while all around them is destroyed. Take care to see you are not like certain codependents who seek approval from the addict for their interventions prior to the implementation of even the simplest strategies. For example, a 45-year-old father, who has demonstrated success as an attorney and church leader might ask a 14-year-old addict (who, likely is under the influence when asked) for ideas on how to deal with abuse problems by saying. "What are we going to do with you?" Even more amazing is that the same capable father will often wait until he gets some kind of permission from his 14-year-old before action is taken.

Unconditional love is more powerful than tough love.

Remember, loving unconditionally is more powerful than implementing tough love. To forgive is more powerful than to punish. Christ who has all power, forgave the woman who committed adultery. Why is that? Because love and forgiveness are very powerful. Keep in mind, *forgiveness is only forgiveness when the codependent has the power to punish, hurt, and ridicule but* chooses *not to*. When unconditional love is woven with tough love, it becomes a mighty offense.

4. LEARN GENERAL PRINCIPLES APPLY SPECIFIC STRATEGIES

A codependent should understand the difference between learning about correct general principles of love and applying specific strategies. Thus far, we have discussed the three correct and general principles that can help codependents deal more effectively with themselves and addicts. It would be impossible to *specifically* say what a codependent should or shouldn't do in any given circumstance. This book stresses applications of *principles* which can only be done individually, in stratagem sessions, when unique circumstances are taken into consideration.

Applying the principle of tough love may be more appropriate at times than applying the principle of unconditional love, and vice versa. Elders Pinegar and Featherstone both had fathers with drinking problems. Elder Featherstone's parents divorced, Elder Pinegar's did not. Today, both are admired general authorities. What may have been a correct specific application of unconditional love in Elder Pinegar's situation may have been in error for the Featherstone family. In the Book of Mormon the righteous often defend their families and their lives through war. However, the people of Ammon would rather haved

> ...sacrifice[d] their lives than even to take the life of their enemy; and they...buried their weapons of war deep in the earth, because of their love towards their brethren (Alma 26:32).

The principle of "thou shalt not kill" is a correct principle, but Nephi was specifically commanded to kill King Laban.

How do codependents know when to apply tough love and when to apply unconditional love? Peace of mind comes when you know you are doing the right thing for the right reason. *Once self-love is established, be receptive to inspiration and acknowledge personal judgement for specific guidance.*

The Lord says:

> For behold, *it is not meet that I should command in all things*; for he that is compelled in all things the same is a slothful and not a wise servant; wherefore he receiveth no reward. Verily I say, men should be anxiously engaged in a good cause, and do many things of their own free will, and bring to pass much righteousness. (D&C 58:26,27, *emphasis added*)

And the Lord goes on to say, "For the power is in them." (D&C 58:28). Joseph Smith taught a similar concept. He said "I teach people correct principles and they govern themselves" (*Journal of Discourses* 10: 57-58). Remember, the Lord is not likely to command and inspire you on each strategy. He's willing to hold on to you with an open hand

and allow you in part to guide your own life according to the principles and wisdom you have obtained.

HINTS FOR EFFECTIVE STRATEGIES

PROPER ASSESSMENT OF SEVERITY

Part of a good strategy requires loved ones to make a judgement about the addict's stage of addiction. The graph below roughly outlines the various stages of addiction. Similar stages exist for all addictions, including addictions for sex, gambling, food, etc. More detailed information on assessing the degree of abuse can be obtained from a local alcohol and drug treatment center, mental health center and your library.

No Use	Experimental Use	Problematic Use	Addictive Use

Strategies to match the severity.
Don't wait until the disease has progressed to the most severe level of addictive use. Select strategies that are appropriate to the addict's level of addiction. For example, if I suspected that my daughter were using alcohol because I found a bottle of beer in her car and she acted funny when she came home the night before, I would likely create a mid-level strategy. If that were the only evidence I had, I would judge my daughter to be somewhere between "experimental use" and "problematic use." A mid-level strategy would include a personal confrontation, which included some moderate consequences. A mid-level strategy does not impose severe consequences like taking

someone to the hospital for in-patient care. *Codependents should gradually increase the severity of the tough love as the addict's addictive behaviors increase.* See Matt. 18:15-17.

LEAST RESTRICTIVE TREATMENT ALTERNATIVE

Generally, after considering the severity factor, loved ones should use the least restrictive treatment alternative first. Often, recovery from addiction will take a long time, usually requiring numerous strategies and numerous interventions. If an in-patient treatment facility is used as a consequence for "addictive use" when the addict is only in "experimental use," what resources are left should the addict later end up in addictive use? Contrary to current advertisements for treatment programs, the disease of addiction is rarely permanently resolved through a single family intervention meeting and subsequent hospital stay. Such interventions are only part of a long and painful recovery process. It is important to accept the fact that *programs don't cure; only God can heal*. However, treatment programs can often facilitate the opening of an addict's heart to God.

Another good reason to choose the least restrictive treatment alternative has to do with the issue of self-love. Loved ones might not have sufficient courage, strength or understanding to follow through on a major intervention, such as kicking the addict out. To start and not follow through with a intervention is a very counter-productive practice. By performing smaller interventions first, you can practice and gain self-love and confidence.

STRATAGEM IS PRIVATE

An addict should not be involved with the formation of a strategy. If a behavioral contract is to be made between codependents and the addict, a strategy session should be held before the contract session with the addict. During the strategy session, the "generals" can discuss the contents of the contract. As shared earlier, a person in the late stages of addiction is unable, because of the disease, to comply with contract agreements anyway and might innocently be set up to fail by loved ones.

Those involved in the strategy sessions should discuss what information is to be disclosed to the addict outside of the meetings. Many of those who have worked with or lived with addicts have learned that if you tell an addict the wall is only twelve feet high, he will get a twelve foot ladder and step over the wall using the top step. Drawing another analogy from the Book of Mormon, it would have been fatal to the Nephites if they had disclosed their defense strategy to the enemy.

A general guideline is: *If in doubt about what information to share with an addict, shut up and say nothing*. Often we feel that sermons, and good communication skills are helpful in dealing with the addict. Perhaps they are in some cases. Generally, however, addicts have turned off their hearts and ears and your verbal efforts are useless. Interestingly enough, they often seem to hear the information necessary to win their battle to continue substance use.

STRATAGEM IS USING A COMBINATION OF TACTICS

Characteristics of almost every addict are dishonesty and cleverness. You will rarely meet an honest practicing addict, or for that matter, a stupid one. As the disease develops, addicts' use begins to influence every part of their lives, including things spiritual, physical, and moral. So, not only are addicts abusing their substance of choice, but also the spiritual substances of which they are made. Thus they begin to lie, or not tell the whole truth, to steal, and practice other negative behaviors. A variety of tactics can be used to intervene with addicts. Be creative. Be flexible. Pray for effective strategies. And remember, strategies should create more pain and suffering for the addict than for you, the codependent.

INTERVENE ON RELATED BEHAVIORS

Strategies may be used on *any* of the negative behaviors exhibited by substance abuser. A loved one does not have to wait until he or she can intervene directly in the alcohol or drug use per se. You can intervene in an addict's temper. For example, your intervention with an addict's defiant door slamming can be as effective a strategy as intervening directly with his alcohol use. Temper outbursts often indicate the disease as well as the substance use itself. Every addict demonstrates a different combination of misbehaviors associated with his or her substance abuse.

USE THE LAW OF MOSES

Select small misbehaviors exhibited by the addict and develop for each brief, intense consequences with which you are able to follow. Apply consequences according to the Law of Moses. These consequences should be applied quietly, quickly, and should result in pain for the addict. For instance, if the addict neglects to feed his pet dog, tell him you will sell the dog if he continues to neglect his responsibility. And then do it. Applying many little interventions on behaviors related to addiction will increase your confidence. Remind yourself frequently that you are responsible to God, not to the addict. Do your best in using fewer words. Often one well planned consequence without words is worth more than several months of counseling.

A REMINDER

Things get worse.
Things get worse with an effective strategy. It's true. Expect conflict when you stop exhibiting the codependent behaviors of rescuing, persecuting, and suffering. The addict's behavior typically gets worse with the behaviors of self-love, unconditional love, and

tough love. Family members and close friends will require time to adjust because it takes both objectivity and courage to initiate effective strategies, knowing that the addict's threats, yelling, and name calling will increase. But be assured that the increasing tension is a sign that you are changing and likely eliminating codependent behaviors. If you are unable to withstand the increased conflict that comes with change, don't plan a strategy. Go back and work on self-love and find a support resource, as taught in Chapter Six.

THE SUNBEAM CHECK

It is important to keep life simple. Earlier we noted that everything we need to know we learned in Primary. "Sunbeam" is the name of the class given to the youngest of the children's Sunday School classes in the LDS Church. Below is a "Sunbeam Check," which can be used to evaluate progress in applying the three attributes of love. A *Sunbeam Check* should be a part of each strategy session.

First.
The Codependents should evaluate their progress in developing self-love by asking themselves the following:
   a. Am I eating and sleeping adequately?
   b. Have I spent time by myself? Have I identified my Mount Sinai, my Forest, my Grove, or my Garden? Have I been there?
   c. Does my self-esteem measure about fifty points on the Self-Love Meter?
   d. Have I set priorities?
   e. Do I have a friend? a support group? some "generals" on my side?

If you can not answer yes to these questions, you have failed the *Sunbeam Check* and should *not* proceed! Nothing is more important than making sure that you have support for the rough times ahead and that you safeguard your salvation, your serenity, your return trip to your Heavenly Father.

Second.

If you have sufficient self-love as determined in the first check, you may move forward to the second phase of the *Sunbeam Check*. Ask yourself: "Have I communicated faith and love to the addict unconditionally through safe-love behaviors?" For example, can you stand to be in the same room as the addict without sending verbal and nonverbal messages of anger and disgust? "Have I left a note acknowledging my love to the addict?" Remember, at times the best safe-love behavior is "keeping your mouth shut" about some of the things the addict is doing wrong. A safe-love behavior could be as simple as sitting next to the addict while watching TV. Part of this includes asking the question "Am I holding on to the addict with an open hand?" Again, unless you have demonstrated a safe-love behavior, you are not ready to move on to tough love.

Third.

To finish the *Sunbeam Check* we ask ourselves: "Is the addict in pain?" The pain experienced by the addict does not necessarily need to be a result of your strategy, but it must occur. If the addict is not suffering, then create a strategy that will cause the addict pain. Administer the Law of Moses quietly and privately with your "generals" and with God.

Codependents should regularly give themselves the *Sunbeam Check* to ensure they are doing what is in the best interest for themselves and the addict. Remember to continue applying the correct principles regardless of the addict's response. Though the addict may continue substance use, even die because of it, you have the assurance that you demonstrated God's kind of love.

AN EXAMPLE FROM THE AUTHOR'S PERSONAL EXPERIENCE

One Friday afternoon while I was in my office, the phone rang. When I answered it a woman's voice was on the other end. She was quite distressed, crying. I discovered she was a Stake Relief Society president from California. She explained, "I went to your workshop at BYU, came home and kicked my son out...but I realize I don't have enough self-love and I'm feeling bad." This good sister was engulfed with guilt, loneliness, and shame. I asked her a few questions and found out her son was thirty-one years old. She told of how he hadn't worked for a long time and that he was drinking. Thinking she was ready for a tough love strategy, she kicked him out. Now she was paying the price for not having developed her self-love first. She explained that she had called her son's friends to make sure he had a place to stay and something to eat. Her tears and pain were intensified. At this point I invited her to do a *Sunbeam Check* with me. We started with simple questions. "How have you been sleeping the last few nights?" I asked. She responded, "Well not very good. I don't get to sleep until about two or three in the morning because I'm worrying too much about my boy." Then came the next question: "How have you been eating?" She answered with, "Not very good. I've been so worried about by son that I haven't felt like eating." As we went on, it became obvious she was more concerned about her son's health than she was about her own. I encouraged her to keep it simple and work on her self-love first.

Effective strategies are determined by your answers to the *Sunbeam Check*, not by what the addict does or doesn't do. Effective strategies judged in this fashion do not fail. They don't fail because the loved ones who participate in the healing process by using strategies eventually obtain emotional and spiritual growth regardless of what the addict may or may not do. Remember, you measure your success in recovery by feedback from God, your "generals," and yourself. Keep in mind that rarely does a single intervention change the life of an addict. And the possibility of relapse into addiction is real and even likely in early years of recovery.

TO MY SON,

IT'S YOUR MOVE

I gave you life,
    but I cannot live it for you.
I can teach you things,
    but I cannot make you learn.
I can give you directions,
    but I cannot always be there to lead you.
I can allow you freedom,
    but I cannot account for it.
I can take you to church,
    but I cannot make you believe.
I can teach you right from wrong,
    but I cannot always decide for you.
I can buy your neat clothes,
    but I cannot make you nice inside.
I can offer you advice,
    but I cannot accept it for you.
I can give you love,
    but I cannot force it upon you.
I can teach you to be a friend
    but I cannot make you one.
I can teach you to share,
    but I cannot make you unselfish.
I can teach you respect,
    but I cannot force you to show honor.
I can grieve about your report card,
    but I cannot make you study.
I can advise you about friends,
    but I cannot choose them for you.
I can teach you about sex and the facts of life,
    but I cannot decide for you.
I can tell you about drinking,
    but I cannot say "no" for you.
I can warn you about drugs,
    but I cannot prevent you from using them.
I can teach about goals and dreams,
    but I cannot achieve them for you.
I can teach you kindness,
    but I cannot force you to be kind.
I can warn you about sin,
    but I cannot make your morals.
I can love you as a son,
    but I cannot place you in God's family.
I can pray for you and your future,
    but I cannot make you walk with God.
I can teach you about Jesus,
    but I cannot make him your Savior.
I can tell you how to live,
    but I cannot give you eternal life.

Thanks for listening.
Good luck with your future.
I love you, son.
Mom

CHAPTER TEN

SUGGESTIONS AND AFTERTHOUGHTS

By Vaughn J. Featherstone

Below is an excerpt from a poem entitled *Stradivarius*.

When any man holds twixt hand and chin
    A violin of mine
They will be glad Stradivarius lived, made violins
    And made them of the best
The Masters only know whose work is good
    And they will choose mine
For while God gives them skill
    I give them instruments to play upon
God choosing me to help him,
    For God could not make Antonio Stradivarius' violin
without Antonio

J.C. Penney is know to have said, that the solution to any problem will come in the form of a human being. The work of reaching out as shepherds is as constant as time. In Ezekiel 34 we read about shepherds in the 34th chapter. Consider these verses:

> Son of man, prophesy against the shepherds of Israel, prophesy, and say unto them, Thus saith the Lord God unto the shepherds; Woe be to the shepherds of Israel that do feed themselves! Should not the shepherds feed the flocks?
>
> Ye eat the fat, and ye clothe you with the wool, ye kill them that are fed: but ye feed not the flock.

> The diseased have ye not strengthened, neither have ye healed that which was sick, neither have ye bound up that which was broken, neither have ye brought again that which was driven away, neither have ye sought that which was lost; but with force and with cruelty have ye ruled them.
>
> And they were scattered, because there is no shepherd: and they became meat to all the beasts of the field, when they were scattered.
>
> My sheep wandered through all the mountains, and upon every high hill: yea, my flock was scattered upon all the face of the earth, and none did search or seek after them. (Ezekiel 34: 2-6)

Whether it be Antonio Stradivarius, a shepherd, or as J.C. Penney said, a human being, there is a need for all of us to help.

Victor Hugo states in *Les Miserables*: "The shepherd does not recoil from the diseased sheep." We must not recoil; we must seek after them, wherever they may wander. Drug addicts have wandered into thickets, dangerous crevices and deep ravines. Shepherds must seek them out. The prophet's words are tender and pitiful: "My flock was scattered upon all the face of the earth and none did search or seek after them."

Here are five suggestions to consider:

I. THE NEED FOR FAMILY MEMBERS AND CHURCH LEADERS TO GET INVOLVED.

In the 1984 edition of the *Resource Manual for Helping Families with Alcohol Problems* church leaders were forewarned:

> Many Church members drink alcoholic beverages [and use other drugs], causing serious problems for themselves and their families...There is an urgent need for concerned leaders and friends to help these people stop drinking [and using other drugs] and keep their family members from starting. (p. 2, © Copyright by The Church of Jesus Christ of Latter-day Saints. Used by permission.)

The Lord must be pleased with priesthood leaders, members, parents, family, and friends who seek after His flock. The accounts in this book encourage people to not give up, to minster to the diseased (addicted) sheep in a Christlike way with unconditional love.

Ted Olsen said:

> And ninety and nine are with dreams content
> But the hope of a world made new
> Is the hundredth man who is grimly bent
> On making the dream come true.

Everyone's involvement is essential. The Church has surely reached out in loving kindness through its many resources, namely manuals, video tapes such as *The Prodigal*, lessons, other curricula, priesthood leader training, *Ensign* and *New Era* articles, conference talks, pamphlets, financial support, and the organization of a Social Services Division in our General Welfare Department.

It has been my personal experience that this wonderful Church has reached out even to the undeserving-those who have rebelled against their parents and the Church, others involved in lying, stealing and deliberate, willful alliance with Satanic forces. Many parents and family members will witness that the Church did not give up, even when all appeared to be lost.

Every priesthood leader has a divine mandate to do all in his power to save every member of the flock, however far he or she may stray. God bless the hundredth man, woman, parent or priesthood leader who gets involved.

II. THE CONCEPT OF CHURCH LEADERS BEING "SHEPHERDS," NOT PHYSICIANS AND PSYCHOLOGISTS.

It seems unfair to expect bishops, Young Men and Young Women presidencies, seminary teachers and other Church leaders to become chemical dependency specialists. In a practical sense, it is unrealistic, given the priorities and time constraints of these leaders, to ask them to become heavily involved in the problems of alcohol and other drug abuse. As servants of Heavenly Father they were called to be "spiritual" leaders. Many seem to be most content and most useful to Him when they pursue what they were called to do, act as spiritual leaders *(shepherds)*, not *physicians*. If needed, they should identify reliable resources in the local area and refer addicts for professional help as needed. King Benjamin helps us to understand the concept of order in the following scriptures:

> And now, for the sake of these things which I have spoke unto you that is, for the sake of retaining a remission of your sins from day to day, that ye may walk guiltless before God I would that ye should impart of your substance to the poor, every man according to that which he hath, such as feeding the hungry, clothing the naked, visiting the sick and administering to their relief, both spiritually and temporally, according to their wants.
>
> And see that all these things are done in wisdom and order; for it is not requisite that a man should run faster than he has strength. And again, it is expedient that he should be diligent, that thereby he might win the prize; therefore, all things must be done in order. (Mosiah 4: 26-27)

Imagine, we must follow King Benjamin's counsel "for the sake of retaining a remission of our sins from day to day." "All these things," he continues, "are done in wisdom and *order*." Order is a critical issue of today. The world has been immersed in knowledge and understanding. The brightest minds are constantly probing unknown areas in the past to find solutions for the future. Specialists and professionals in the field of chemical addiction may be required to assist those suffering from alcohol and drug related problems.

As members of the Church our responsibilities rest in providing loving, caring support, in reaching out and searching after as shepherds do, in exercising the greatest acts of charity we have ever been called upon to perform. We must always and ever remember the promise that "charity never faileth" (1 Cor. 13).

We cannot be the specialists; we must be the watchmen, the shepherds, the nurturers. And we must never, never, never give up. God bless those who may not have all the technical knowledge and skills, but who surely have the love and spiritual strength to help.

III. CHURCH LEADERS IN A UNIQUE POSITION TO HELP.

Church leaders are in a unique position to be involved in the daily personal lives of members. They have the trust of thousands of LDS families, many of which are experiencing the "highs" and the "lows" of chemical addiction. These leaders' unique position with LDS families and their willingness to understand the alcohol and drug issue offer a positive outlook on the prevention and intervention of LDS chemical addiction.

Leaders who are called, ordained and set apart are endowed with many blessings. These are gifts of the Spirit which can be called upon at the precise time of need. Section 46 of the Doctrine and Covenants, verse 27, states:

> And unto the bishop of the church, and unto such as God shall appoint and ordain to watch over the church and to be elders unto the church, are to have it given unto them to discern all those gifts lest there shall be any among you professing and yet be not of God.

Imagine what it means to "have it given to discern all those gifts." The God of heaven does not call us to serve His people and then leave us without direct guidance. Those who humbly and meekly serve and submit to His greater will, always have the needed gifts when they are truly warranted. Verses 11 through 30 in this same section tell of the kindness, the goodness, and the tenderness of our God when his children humbly submit themselves to the work they are called to perform.

I have a witness that direct revelation and inspiration accompany great, noble priesthood leaders who love and serve their fellowmen. Remember, brethren and sisters, you who lead are in a unique position to help.

IV. CHURCH LEADERS AND FAMILY MEMBERS NEED TO DEMONSTRATE THE KIND OF LOVE SHOWN IN PRODIGAL SON (TOUGH LOVE) AS WELL AS GOOD SAMARITAN KIND OF LOVE (UNCONDITIONAL LOVE).

One of the greatest challenges of dealing with the chemically dependent is changing the role from that of "advocate" of total abstinence to that of a "fellowshipper" of the addict-to change from one who gives only compassion to one who confronts the issue; from one who patiently endures to one who anxiously intervenes. This is needless to say, a difficult task, but Church leaders should know they are innocently providing "unhelpful help" if they always and only demonstrate unconditional love in the life of an addict.

I have been involved as an advocate and as a fellowshipper. I can witness to you that being an advocate allows us to stay in our comfort zone. It is simply a matter of putting into word and practice the doctrines and principles we have been taught all our lives. As advocates we teach and say all the right things, we promise our prayers and support, yet we do not get involved.

General Lucius Paulus, sometimes called Macedonicus, explains the true concept of fellowshipping:

> Commanders should be counselled chiefly by persons of known talent, by those who have made the art of war their particular study, and whose knowledge is derived from experience, by those who are present at the scene of action, who see the enemy, who see the advantages that occasions offer, and who, like people embarked in the same ship are sharers of the danger.
>
> If, therefore, anyone thinks himself qualified to give advice respecting the war which I am about to conduct, let him not refuse his assistance to the state, but let him come with me into Macedonia.
>
> He shall be furnished with a ship, a tent, even his travelling charges will be defrayed, but if he thinks this too much trouble, and prefers the repose of a city life to the toils of war, let him not on land assume the office of a pilot. The city in itself furnishes abundance of topics for conversation; let it confine its passion for talking to its own precincts and rest assured that we shall pay no attention to any counsel but such as shall be framed within our camp. (General Lucius Aemilius Paulus

surnamed Macedonicus, Roman General and Patrician, C. 229-160 B.C.)

Fellowshippers qualify because they get involved, they see the evening up close and share of the same dangers.

Fellowshipping involves confrontation, tough love, and a desire to assist the addict in making the necessary change. Fellowshipping requires anxious intervention and great charity. There is no substitute for involvement if it is done in a Christlike way, which requires an application of unconditional love, charity, chastising, rebuking, tenderness, gentleness, love unfeigned, persuasion, suffering, anguishing, and patience. It is a Christlike mixture of all of the ingredients of tough love combined with unconditional Christlike charity.

V. A THOUGHT ABOUT "MORALISTIC SERMONS."

Research has suggested that parents, teachers and church leaders have not been seen by adolescents as credible sources of information about alcohol and drugs. That is, church leaders and parents typically teach only the last stage of addiction and its evils while their youth see the first stage of addiction and its pleasure (See Chapter One). These type of moralistic sermons against alcohol and drugs using *only* scare tactics are likely to result in adolescents' dismissing the lecture and turning to their friends for more information. Church leaders and parents must be sure to teach young people correct principles and then recognize that each individual has moral agency to decide.

For the most part, sin is pleasurable. It appeals to our fleshly appetites. Life's battle is a struggle between discipline and indulgence- indulgences like food, sex, vices, and pornography which bring pleasure and momentary satisfaction.

Discipline requires control, discipleship, trust, integrity, and honesty as well as other character traits. Youth and those enslaved by addiction need to hear and understand not just the final consequence of indulgence, but the deceptive, flagrant snares that trap them. They need to know that their leaders understand temptation and sin are pleasurable in the beginning. They need to know how Satan uses his subtlety to carefully lead them down to hell. They must also be taught there is always a consequence for transgression, that they have control over their decisions but not over the consequences. Consequences can carry a lifetime of sorrow, regret, disease, physical impairment, and mental impairment.

Church leaders need to warn, plead, beg, and teach the youth to listen and heed their counsel. Few are prepared for the consequences of sin. As they would do anything righteous to save their youth from "physical" danger, so should they do everything in their power to save the youth from "spiritual" danger.

Moral agency belongs to everyone individually. Each can influence and be influenced. The leader's responsibility is to influence for good, to be an example of virtue, honor, control and the eventual consequence of a good Christian life. God has promised pleasures and blessings beyond any dreams and expectations for those who simply are obedient and keep His commandments.

APPENDIX A

RESOURCES

HOLD ON TO HOPE VIDEO

HOLD ON TO HOPE is a 34-minute video that takes a spiritual look at chemical addiction and recovery. For many involved with chemical addiction and alcohol dependency, there is an overwhelming feeling of hopelessness. They feel there is absolutely "no way out." They would stop if they could, but they have lost the ability to choose for themselves. For addicts, the question of "choice" has been answered; the choice is no longer theirs. Addicts, and their loved ones, may carry the extra burden of living contrary to religious and spiritual beliefs. These spiritual concerns must be addressed and understood if the addict is to be helped. Understanding is the pass-key that opens the door to recovery. As the addicts gain understanding, they let go of the guilt and shame and can then truly "hold on to hope" with both hands.

This video dramatizes LDS aspects of addiction, codependence, and recovery discussed in this book. A viewer's guide accompanies the video, assisting the audience in gaining maximum benefit from the video. For additional information, contact:

Lorien Productions
P.O. Box 39
Bountiful, UT 84011
801/298-2858

RESOURCE MANUAL FOR HELPING FAMILIES WITH ALCOHOL PROBLEMS

This manual is published by the Church of Jesus Christ of Latter-day Saints and is tailored to meet the organization's structure and the needs believed to be unique to its members. The 128-page manual presents the ideas of using resource persons. These resource persons are called by Church leaders and are instructed to use the information provided in the manual. They, in turn help individuals and families affected by alcohol abuse within their local congregations. The LDS Church is in the process of rewriting this manual. Changes will include, among others things, discussing illicit drugs as well as alcohol. This manual can be ordered through the LDS Church Distribution Center in Salt Lake City, Utah. The catalogue number is PGSC6258.

S.A.V.E. (AN LDS-TAILORED 12-STEP SUPPORT GROUP).

"I had reached the point in my life where there were two ways to go. I could accept God and live, or go on as I was and die," said Carl, a recovering alcoholic and member of S.A.V.E. (Substance Abuse Volunteer Efforts). Carl is living proof that S.A.V.E. does just what the name says. The soft-spoken 30-year-old man was very earnest as he related his experience with the group. "There was just no place for me to go. I was born and raised a member of the LDS Church and knew that alcohol use was wrong. I couldn't go back to church because I felt I didn't belong because of my Word of Wisdom problem. I tried to talk to the bishop, but I'm not sure he could understand me. I had been drinking about a fifth of vodka a day for several years, but I knew it was time to change or die. I went to A.A. meetings and they really helped, but something was still missing. I was unable to talk about God and my Church. Then I heard about S.A.V.E. and began attending regularly. I gained hope that there was a way back at my first meeting. I've been sober for two years now and enjoy the brotherhood at priesthood meeting."

That's an example of the many stories by persons who have found hope in S.A.V.E. Dr. Rick H., S.A.V.E. Co-founder, was an alcohol counselor at a government clinic in Utah during 1982. He recognized the difficulty LDS substance abusers and their family members had in recovering from addiction. S.A.V.E. was organized in 1983 as a private non-profit corporation within the state of Utah. S.A.V.E. members joined together as a small group of substance abusers and surrounding family members to discuss their concerns and problems as they related to substance abuse and the LDS Church.

Family members and friends who care about a drug and alcohol abuser are encouraged to attend S.A.V.E. support group meetings and obtain help for themselves. Connie was married to an alcoholic for 20 years. "I really thought it was my fault...if there wasn't something wrong with me he wouldn't drink. Things got so bad that I forgot who I was. I was sick all the time. I had a big knot in the middle of my stomach day after day, wondering what I was going to do next. During this time I always went to Church and held Church positions. I felt no one could understand my desperation and hopelessness." The mother of five children went on to say "I found S.A.V.E. and learned that I could find peace and serenity."

S.A.V.E. respects the spiritual principles of the LDS Church. The support meetings are patterned after the 12-step program of A.A. S.A.V.E. has received formal permission from Alcoholics Anonymous World Service Center to adapt the 12-steps and the 12 Traditions to a format which accommodate the needs of LDS persons. It is the only organization that has adopted the Alcoholics Anonymous program to meet the needs of a specific religious denomination. S.A.V.E. provides weekly support meetings for substance abusers and codependents. These meetings are held at various locations throughout local communities. S.A.V.E. codependents consist of relatives and friends of substance abusers and include adult children of the chemically dependent.

Sherilyn reminisces about living with an alcoholic father. "My father died of liver cancer when I was a sophomore in high school. It took twenty more years after this for my family to verbalize his addiction to alcohol." Sherilyn recalls "...spending much of my life trying to be *perfect* in order to *fix* my family." "I tried to *control* everything and everyone to get my family to be a perfect Mormon family who would dress in white and sit on the front row at Church." Sherilyn, now married and a mother of four, attends S.A.V.E. meetings for adult children of alcoholics. "My Higher Power gave me the gift of S.A.V.E. and the 12-steps and I am able to finish, and let go, and turn over to God my family-of-origin issues."

S.A.V.E. is indeed a very ambitious organization and, many believe an inspired program. S.A.V.E. members come from all walks of life. There is no charge to attend. The anonymity of S.A.V.E. members is one of the 12 Traditions. As such, the identity of all who choose to attend is kept confidential. Hundreds of S.A.V.E. members, with assistance from their Higher Power have broken out of the hopeless guilt-ridden rut that afflicts so many members of the LDS Church who find themselves in this type of difficulty. For additional information contact:

S.A.V.E.
2568 Washington Blvd.
Ogden, UT 84401
801/621-7283

INDEX

—A—

Abusive 35
Acceptance 11, 51, 75
Adaptive behaviors 27
Addiction vii-viii, 2-5, 7-9, 11-17, 19, 25, 27-29, 32, 34-35, 37-38, 46-49, 52, 53, 67, 75, 79, 81, 95, 98, 102, 104-108, 110, 115-16, 118, 121, 126-27, 129, 131, 133
Addiction Cycle 1, 3, 16
Addiction, Healthy 15
Addiction, Unhealthy 15
Adjusting 27, 29, 38, 53
Agency vii, 13-14, 16, 36, 73, 80, 84, 91, 96-97, 129-30
Alcohol vii-viii, 1-5, 8, 10, 11, 13, 15, 17, 19-23, 25, 27, 30, 34, 39, 43, 45, 47-52, 63, 70, 77, 79-80, 83-84, 89-90, 102, 106-107, 115, 118, 124-27, 129, 131-34
Anonymity vii, 21, 134

—B—

Benson, Ezra Taft 2
Bottom viii, 48, 91, 95

—C—

Carmack, John 34, 89
Change iv, vii, 8-11, 14, 19-21, 25, 29, 34, 45, 47, 50, 64, 73, 75, 85, 88, 90, 92, 103, 111, 119, 121, 128-29, 132
Church 1, 3-6, 8-9, 11-12, 15-16, 19-23, 25, 27, 30-35, 39-43, 45, 48, 51, 53-54, 56, 58, 60-61, 64-68, 75, 83-84, 90, 92, 96-97, 99, 106-107, 113, 119, 122, 124-30, 132-34

Co-alcoholic 29
Codependence 33-34, 37, 45, 49, 54, 57, 60-61, 67-68, 70, 74, 76, 105, 109, 131
Codependency 27, 29, 31, 36-37, 45, 47, 50, 54, 62-63, 67, 100, 108, 110
Commandments 1, 2, 5, 7, 55, 64, 99, 130
Communicate 76, 120
Consequences 1, 2, 5-7, 12, 16, 29-31, 35, 45, 50, 52, 54, 88-90, 92, 98-99, 101, 109, 115, 118, 130
Control viii, 25, 33-34, 36-37, 45, 47, 48, 50, 73, 88, 96, 129-30, 133
Covering up 29, 31, 89
Crack 2

—D—

Defeat 36
Denial viii, 29-30, 46-47, 49
Denying 29-30, 89
Depression 16, 36, 39
Disease vii-viii, 1-2, 13, 15-16, 21-22, 24-25, 27, 29, 32, 53, 74, 79, 82, 84, 95, 98, 102, 115-18, 124-25, 130
Disobedience 5, 8, 13, 16
Distress 13, 27, 29, 35, 69, 120
Drug viii, 1-5, 8-11, 13-16, 20-22, 27, 30, 32-33, 36, 39, 45-47, 63, 84, 89-90, 96, 107, 115, 118, 122, 124-27, 129, 132-33

—E—

Enable 29, 37, 88

Esteem 4, 9, 36, 54, 60, 62, 68-69, 111, 119
Eternal 52-53, 67, 80, 83-84, 96, 98, 111, 122
Eternal family 84

—F—

Faith 1, 25, 52-53, 60, 68, 77, 81, 85, 95-98, 100, 103, 120
Featherstone, Vaughn J. vii, 39, 114, 123
Forgiveness 78-79, 113
Freedom 13, 36-37, 62, 80, 99, 102, 107, 122
Friends 9-10, 14-15, 19, 25, 32-33, 37, 42, 46, 48, 51, 68, 118, 121-22, 124, 133

—G—

God's love 54, 69, 86
Grief 37
Guilt 5, 11-12, 23, 30, 33, 35, 43, 48, 50, 54, 66, 75, 79-80, 83, 89, 100-102, 107, 121, 126, 131, 134

—H—

Haight, David B. 27
High 2-4, 8, 12-13, 60, 127
Hope vii-viii, 21, 25, 39, 42-43, 52, 66, 74-75, 84, 98, 100, 113, 125, 131-32
Hostility 9-10

—I—

Immoral 1, 2, 5, 10, 12
Intervene vii-viii, 16, 83, 97, 102, 117-18, 128
Intervention viii, 17, 23-24, 54, 64, 81, 95, 99-102, 106, 111, 113, 116, 118, 121, 127, 129
Intoxication 10, 75, 102

Irrational Behaviors 34

—J—

Joy 3-4, 7-9, 12, 67
Justice 36, 97, 99, 101

—K—

Kimball, Spencer W. 61, 70

—L—

Larsen, Dean L. 60, 101
Law of Chastity 1, 5-6, 14, 94
Law of Moses 98-101, 118, 120
Lee, George P. 34
Liberty 106-107
Love Formula 55-56, 60, 68
Lying 9, 11, 15, 29, 32, 89, 99, 125

—M—

Marijuana 2, 7-9, 13
Martyr 29

—N—

Narcissism 57, 60, 70

—P—

Packer, Boyd K. 16
Pain 2-3, 7-9, 11-14, 20-23, 30, 32, 45-47, 50, 75, 78-80, 89-90, 92-95, 98, 100-101, 106, 116, 117-18, 120-21
Paraphernalia 10, 30
PCP 2
Persecuting Behaviors 28, 32-33, 73, 86
Persecutor 29
Personal vii, 14, 17, 19, 33, 36, 39, 45, 57, 63-70, 76, 84-85, 87, 100, 102, 107-108, 114-15, 120, 125, 127

Pornography 3-5, 7-8, 13-14, 33, 107, 129
Powerless 23, 36, 81, 88, 95-97, 108
Priorities 66, 119, 125
Prodigal Son 90-92, 95, 109, 128
Punishment 109

—R—

Rationalize 11, 37
Rebellion 6
Recovery 16-17, 21, 23-25, 49-50, 54, 60, 67-69, 74, 76, 78, 80-81, 84, 86, 95, 97-98, 103, 110, 116, 121, 131
Refiner's Fire 92, 94-95
Reproving 111
Rescuing Behaviors 27, 29, 32-34, 89
Resentment 33, 78-79, 81, 100
Richards, Stephen L. 1
Risk factor 4
Roadblocks 70

—S—

Safe Love 81-82, 86, 94, 113, 120
Salvation 37, 57, 62-64, 66, 83, 87, 110, 119
Samaritan 73-74, 86-87, 90-92, 128
Season 3-4, 7-8, 13, 15
Self-love 53-55, 57-60, 63-66, 68-70, 74, 110-11, 114, 116, 118-21
Self-reliance 36-37, 61, 63
Self-worth 67, 73, 89
Selfish 54, 57, 60, 70, 76
Selfless 57, 60
Slavery 16
Spiritual Ruin 4, 15
Stage 3-5, 7-9, 11-16, 29, 31-36, 54, 75, 79, 102-103, 106, 115-16, 129

Step 24-25, 69, 73-75, 117
Step, Twelve 21, 49, 51, 105, 132-34
Strategies viii, 64, 101, 105, 108, 110, 113, 115-19, 121
Strategy 54, 82, 99-100, 102, 105, 108, 110-11, 113-21
Substance abuse vii, 9, 29-33, 35, 37, 81, 83, 100, 118, 132-33
Suffering Behaviors 28, 34, 36, 54, 69
Sunbeam 119-21
Support 8, 49, 54, 56, 61, 67-68, 76, 94, 106, 111, 119, 125-26, 128, 132-33

—T—

Threats 14, 33, 90, 119
Tolerance 8, 10, 22
Tough love 79, 81, 87, 89-103, 110-14, 116, 118, 120-21, 128-29
Treasure 5, 53, 55, 60, 66, 70

—U—

Unconditional Love 73-83, 85-87, 90-91, 110-11, 112-14, 118, 125, 128-29
Unfaithfulness 98

—V—

Values 8, 9
Victim viii, 29, 52, 76, 91

—W—

Warning 2, 4, 9
Word of Wisdom 1-2, 5-6, 14, 16, 83, 94, 132
Worry 35-36, 45, 48, 51, 62, 91, 121
Worth 68-69, 83-85, 98
Worthiness 83